Jakarta Struts
Pocket Reference

T0260464

Chuck Cavaness and Brian Keeton

O'REILLY®

Beijing · Boston · Farnham · Sebastopol · Tokyo

Jakarta Struts Pocket Reference
by Chuck Cavaness and Brian Keeton

Published by O'Reilly & Associates, Inc., 1005 Gravenstein Highway North, Sebastopol, CA 95472.

O'Reilly & Associates books may be purchased for educational, business, or sales promotional use. Online editions are also available for most titles (*safari.oreilly.com*). For more information, contact our corporate/institutional sales department: (800) 998-9938 or *corporate@oreilly.com*.

Editor:	Brett McLaughlin
Production Editor:	Genevieve d'Entremont
Cover Designer:	Emma Colby
Interior Designer:	David Futato

Printing History:

June 2003:   First Edition.

978-0-596-00519-1
[LSI]

Contents

Part II. Using Struts ActionForms

Part III.   Built-in Action Classes

Part IV. Tag Reference

Part V. Resources

Jakarta Struts
Pocket Reference

Introduction

Jakarta Struts is an open source, Java™-based framework for building web applications. The framework was developed by the Apache Software Foundation and is housed online at *http://jakarta.apache.org/struts/*. Recognizing that every developer has a standard set of classes, tools, and utilities that are common to even the most divergent web applications, the Struts project has sought to take these commonalities and create from them a reusable and sturdy starting point for web application development.

From a technical standpoint, Struts is based upon the Model 2 approach, which is a slight variation on the Model-View-Controller (MVC) design pattern. Struts provides a generic controller that works well with any application, and then provides simple hooks into a variety of view technologies, such as JavaServer Pages, servlets, XSLT-based frameworks, and other Jakarta presentation frameworks such as Velocity templates. The controller can also easily interact with a variety of model components, including Enterprise JavaBeans™, JDBC, and object-relational mapping technologies. It is no exaggeration to say that Jakarta Struts can handle nearly any combination of model and view technologies you could dream up—and it handles the task seamlessly.

While there are literally hundreds of ways to build a web application, Jakarta Struts takes the most common components of all these solutions and provides them to the developer, prebuilt, documented, and ready for use. Logging, internationalization, debugging, validation, and more are all provided with a simple download of the Struts framework. It is no wonder that Struts (and the books that document it) are becoming the hottest thing going in the Java technology space.

However, as with any complex framework, there is more to using it than binary objects, source code, or even comprehensive user manuals. There are those repetitive tasks that involve this particular method, or that particular set of arguments, that take up space in the memory banks of every developer. As you begin to take advantage of Struts, from its simplest to its most complex functionality, you will find yourself trying to remember exactly which tags do what and where to place that XML element in your Struts configuration file. While you could certainly page through a 500 page tome on Jakarta Struts and find your answer, this book takes a more practical approach (and one that is quite a bit smaller!). The authors have provided a quick reference to all the common tasks you'll find in Struts, allowing you to take nothing more than your Struts experience and this book in a back pocket to client engagements. Whether it's a default action class or the location of Struts add-on classes, this pocket reference has it all, in a size that even today's airlines won't give you trouble over. We hope you'll enjoy the reference and find it helpful in your daily Struts programming.

Conventions Used in This Book

The following typographical conventions are used in this book:

Italic

> Used to indicate new terms, URLs, filenames, file extensions, and directories.

`Constant width`

> Indicates code lines that should be typed verbatim; names and keywords in Java programs, including method names, variable names, and class names; and XML element names, tags, attributes, and values.

`Constant width bold`

> Used in code examples to emphasize lines of particular note.

`Constant width italic`

> Used in examples and tables to show text that should be replaced with user-supplied values.

NOTE

Indicates a tip, suggestion, or general note.

WARNING

Indicates a warning or caution.

PART I

Configuring Struts

For every Struts application, there are at least two configuration files that must be present: the web application deployment descriptor and a Struts configuration file. This part discusses each one in turn.

Configuring web.xml

Each Struts application must include a web application deployment descriptor named *web.xml*, which must be placed in the *WEB-INF* directory. The web container reads and parses the descriptor file at startup and uses the settings to configure the runtime environment for the installed web application.

Although there are many available configuration settings that can affect the container's runtime environment, it's not necessary to configure all of the settings for a Struts application. In many cases, the absence of a setting or the container's default values will be sufficient. Only those settings that pertain to Struts applications will be examined here.

For Struts applications, the following configuration settings are typically configured within the *web.xml* file:

- Struts `ActionServlet` settings
- Initialization parameters
- `load-on-startup` settings
- Welcome file list
- Tag libraries mappings

Configuring the Struts ActionServlet

The Struts ActionServlet is designed to receive all incoming requests for the web application. Two steps are necessary when configuring the ActionServlet in the *web.xml* file. The first step is to use the servlet element to configure the fully qualified Java class name of the ActionServlet:

```
<web-app>
 <servlet>
  <servlet-name>storefront</servlet-name>
  <servlet-class>org.apache.struts.action.ActionServlet
  </servlet-class>
 </servlet>
</web-app>
```

In this *web.xml* example, the servlet element declares two child elements, servlet-name and servlet-class. The servlet-class element specifies the fully qualified class that will function as the front controller for the Struts application. The Java class specified must be a descendant of the org.apache.struts.action.ActionServlet. If you don't have a need for specialized behavior, you can safely use the default controller as shown in the previous *web.xml* fragment.

The servlet-name element acts as a logical name for the ActionServlet. It is used in other elements within the deployment descriptor. You can specify whatever value you like here, as long as it adheres to the Servlet Specification naming guidelines.

The second step required to configure the ActionServlet is to inform the web container which URL requests should be directed to the ActionServlet controller. This is done using the servlet-mapping element:

```
<web-app>
 <servlet>
  <servlet-name>storefront</servlet-name>
  <servlet-class>
   org.apache.struts.action.ActionServlet
  </servlet-class>
 </servlet>
```

```
<servlet-mapping>
  <servlet-name>storefront</servlet-name>
  <url-pattern>*.do</url-pattern>
</servlet-mapping>
</web-app>
```

In the example `servlet` and `servlet-mapping` elements shown, any request containing a URL that matches *.do* would be processed by the servlet named *storefront*.

Declaring Initialization Parameters

Within the `servlet` element, you can specify multiple `init-param` elements. The parameters listed in Table 1 are used by the `ActionServlet` to configure the Struts application runtime environment.

Table 1. ActionServlet initialization parameters

Name	Purpose
config	Comma-separated list of context-relative path(s) to the XML resource(s) containing the configuration information for the default module. The default value is */WEB-INF/struts-config.xml*.
config/${module}	Comma-separated list of context-relative path(s) to the XML resource(s) containing the configuration information for the module that will use the specified prefix (/${module}). This can be repeated as many times as required for multiple modules.
convertNull	Forces simulation of the Struts 1.0 behavior when populating forms. If set to true, the numeric Java wrapper class types such as java.lang.Integer default to null (rather than 0). The default value is false.
rulesets	Comma-delimited list of fully qualified class names of additional org.apache.commons.digester. RuleSet instances that should be added to the Digester and that will process the Struts configuration files. By default, only the RuleSet for the standard configuration elements is loaded.
validating	Specifies whether a validating XML parser should be used to process the configuration file. The default value is true.

To configure one of the initialization parameters, an init-param element is added within the servlet element as shown here:

```
<web-app>
 <servlet>
  <servlet-name>storefront</servlet-name>
  <servlet-class>org.apache.struts.action.ActionServlet
  </servlet-class>
  <init-param>
   <param-name>config</param-name>
   <param-value>/WEB-INF/struts-config.xml</param-value>
  </init-param>
 </servlet>

 <servlet-mapping>
  <servlet-name>storefront</servlet-name>
  <url-pattern>*.do</url-pattern>
 </servlet-mapping>
</web-app>
```

You can add as many init-param elements as the application requires.

Using the load-on-startup Setting

The load-on-startup element directs the web container to instantiate an instance of the specified servlet-class and invoke the init( ) method.

```
<web-app>
 <servlet>
  <servlet-name>storefront</servlet-name>
  <servlet-class>org.apache.struts.action.ActionServlet
  </servlet-class>
  <load-on-startup>1</load-on-startup>
 </servlet>

 <servlet-mapping>
  <servlet-name>storefront</servlet-name>
  <url-pattern>*.do</url-pattern>
 </servlet-mapping>
</web-app>
```

The integer value specified in the load-on-startup element tells the container the order in which the servlets should be called, in case there are more than one specified in the *web.xml* file. If the value is negative or not present, the container is free to load the servlets in any order.

WARNING

For Struts applications, it's essential that you include the load-on-startup element to ensure the proper initialization of resources.

Setting Up the Welcome File List

The welcome-file-list element specifies a starting page for the web application other than the default for the container. For example, if you want the page *index.jsp* to be executed when a client enters the root URL for the web application, add the following XML element:

```
<web-app>
 <servlet>
  <servlet-name>storefront</servlet-name>
  <servlet-class>org.apache.struts.action.ActionServlet
  </servlet-class>
  <load-on-startup>1</load-on-startup>
 </servlet>

 <servlet-mapping>
  <servlet-name>storefront</servlet-name>
  <url-pattern>*.do</url-pattern>
 </servlet-mapping>

 <welcome-file-list>
  <welcome-file>index.jsp</welcome-file>
 </welcome-file-list>
</web-app>
```

Since all requests should go through the Struts controller (in order for the correct module to be selected), it's sometimes necessary to use a combination of the welcome-file-list and the forward JSP tag to invoke an Action using the default startup page. For example, the *index.jsp* page included in the previous welcome-file element might look like:

```
<%@ taglib uri="/WEB-INF/struts-logic.tld" prefix="logic" %>
<html>
 <body>
  <logic:forward name="welcome"/>
 </body>
</html>
```

In this example, when the container invokes the *index.jsp* page, the Action named welcome will be invoked.

Configuring the Tag Libraries

The Struts framework includes several JSP tag libraries that can be used within your JSPs. In order for the container to find the descriptor files for a tag library, include a taglib element in the *web.xml* file for each library:

```
<web-app>
 <servlet>
  <servlet-name>storefront</servlet-name>
  <servlet-class>org.apache.struts.action.ActionServlet
  </servlet-class>
  <load-on-startup>1</load-on-startup>
 </servlet>

 <servlet-mapping>
  <servlet-name>storefront</servlet-name>
  <url-pattern>*.do</url-pattern>
 </servlet-mapping>

 <welcome-file-list>
  <welcome-file>index.jsp</welcome-file>
 </welcome-file-list>

 <taglib>
  <taglib-uri>/WEB-INF/struts-html.tld</taglib-uri>
  <taglib-location>/WEB-INF/struts-html.tld
  </taglib-location>
 </taglib>
```

```
<taglib>
 <taglib-uri>/WEB-INF/struts-bean.tld</taglib-uri>
 <taglib-location>/WEB-INF/struts-bean.tld
 </taglib-location>
</taglib>

<taglib>
 <taglib-uri>/WEB-INF/struts-logic.tld</taglib-uri>
 <taglib-location>/WEB-INF/struts-logic.tld
 </taglib-location>
</taglib>
</web-app>
```

The Struts Configuration Files

The Struts framework uses an XML-based configuration file to declaratively configure all aspects of the Struts application. By default, this file is named *struts-config.xml*, although you can call it whatever you like. The file is normally placed within the *WEB-INF* directory. The location can actually be specified within the *web.xml* file using the `config` initialization parameter.

Using Multiple Struts Configuration Files

Each Struts application can have one or more Struts configuration files per module. For each module, the framework parses the separate configuration files, merges all of the configuration settings in memory, and presents them as a single set of instructions for the application. The configuration settings for each module are kept separate from one another.

To configure multiple Struts configuration files for a single module, include the filenames (separated by a comma) within the `config` initialization parameter element. For example, the following XML fragment illustrates adding two different configuration files for the default module:

```
<init-param>
 <param-name>config</param-name>
 <param-value>
   /WEB-INF/struts-config.xml,/WEB-INF/struts-config2.xml
 </param-value>
</init-param>
```

The data-sources Element

The data-sources element allows you to set up a datasource that you can utilize from within the Struts framework. The data-sources element contains zero or more data-source elements as shown here:

```
<!ELEMENT data-sources (data-source*)>
```

Table 2 lists the data-source element's attributes.

Table 2. The data-source element's attributes

Name	Description
className	The implementation class of the configuration bean that will hold the datasource information. If specified, it must be a descendant of org.apache.struts.config.DataSourceConfig, which is the default value.
key	The servlet context attribute under which this datasource object will be stored. The default value is Globals.DATA_SOURCE_KEY.
type	The fully qualified Java class name of the datasource implementation class. The class specified here must implement the javax.sql.DataSource interface and be configurable from JavaBeans properties. The default value is org.apache.struts.util.GenericDataSource.

The data-source element allows for multiple set-property elements to be specified:

```
<!ELEMENT data-source (set-property*)>
```

The set-property element configures properties that are specific to your datasource implementation.

The following data-sources example illustrates how to set up a datasource that utilizes an Oracle database:

```
<data-sources>
 <data-source>
  <set-property property="autoCommit" value="false"/>
  <set-property property="description"
    value="Oracle Datasource"/>
  <set-property
    property="driverClass"
    value="oracle.jdbc.driver.OracleDriver"/>
  <set-property property="maxCount" value="5"/>
  <set-property property="minCount" value="1"/>
  <set-property property="user" value="scott"/>
  <set-property property="password" value="tiger"/>
  <set-property
    property="url"
    value="jdbc:oracle:thin:@localhost:1521:DEV"/>
 </data-source>
</data-sources>
```

By default, the Struts framework will utilize the DBCP component from the Commons project. By using the type attribute, you can substitute other datasource implementations. For example, the following data-source fragment shows how to use the datasource implementation included with the Oracle JDBC driver:

```
<data-sources>
 <data-source type="oracle.jdbc.pool.OracleDataSource">
```

```
<set-property property="description"
  value="Oracle Datasource"/>
<set-property
  property="driverClass"
  value="oracle.jdbc.driver.OracleDriver"/>
<set-property property="user" value="scott"/>
<set-property property="password" value="tiger"/>

<set-property
  property="url"
  value="jdbc:oracle:thin:@localhost:1521:DEV"/>
</data-source>
</data-sources>
```

The form-beans Element

The form-beans element configures multiple ActionForm
classes for use within the Action classes and the view. Within
the form-beans section, you can configure zero or more form-
bean child elements. Each form-bean element represents a
physical ActionForm class and has several child elements:

```
<!ELEMENT form-bean (icon?, display-name?, description?,
set-property*, form-property*)>
```

Each form-bean element has four attributes that you can
specify (see Table 3).

Table 3. The form-bean attributes

Name	Description
className	If you don't want to use the standard configuration bean org.apache.struts.config.FormBeanConfig, you can specify your own class here. It must be a descendant of the FormBeanConfig class.
dynamic	You no longer have to set this attribute. It's included here because it was deprecated during the 1.1 Beta process. The framework determines this value based on the value of the type attribute. If the class specified in the type attribute is a descendant of the DynaActionForm class, the dynamic property will be set to true.

Table 3. The form-bean attributes (continued)

Name	Description
name	The unique identifier for this form bean; referenced by the `action` element to specify which form bean to use with its request. This value is required and must be unique within a module.
type	The fully qualified name of a Java class that extends the Struts `ActionForm` class. This attribute is required.

The following form-beans element illustrates how to specify a nondynamic ActionForm.

```
<form-beans>
 <form-bean
   name="loginForm"
   type="com.cavaness.banking.web.user.LoginForm"/>
</form-beans>
```

You can pass one or more dynamic properties to the org. apache.struts.action.DynaActionForm class using the form-property element. Dynamic properties are supported only when the type attribute of the surrounding form-bean element is org.apache.struts.action.DynaActionForm or a descendant class. Each form-property element also has five attributes that you can specify (see Table 4).

Table 4. The attributes of the form-property element

Name	Description
className	If you don't want to use the standard configuration bean `org.apache.struts.config.FormPropertyConfig`, you can specify your own class here.
initial	A string representation of the initial value for this property. Property values are initialized based on standard Java conventions.
name	The name of the property being described by this element. This attribute is required.
size	The number of array elements to create if the value of the `type` attribute specifies an array. The default value is 0.
type	The fully qualified Java class name of the implementation class of this bean property, optionally followed by "[ ]" to indicate that this field is indexed. This attribute is required.

The following form-bean fragment illustrates using the form-property element to specify a dynamic ActionForm:

```
<form-bean
  name="checkoutForm"
    type="org.apache.struts.action.DynaActionForm">
    <form-property name="firstName"
      type="java.lang.String"/>
    <form-property name="lastName"
      type="java.lang.String"/>
    <form-property name="age" type="java.lang.Integer"
      initial="18"/>
</form-bean>
```

The global-exceptions Element

The global-exceptions section allows you to configure exception handlers declaratively. The global-exceptions element can contain zero or more exception elements:

```
<!ELEMENT global-exceptions (exception*)>
```

The exception element can also be specified in the action element. If an exception element is configured for the same type of exception both as a global exception and within an action element, the action level will take precedence. If no exception element mapping is found at the action level, the framework will then look for an exception mapping defined for the exception's parent class. Eventually, if a handler is not found, a ServletException or IOException will be thrown, depending on the type of the original exception.

The declaration of the exception element illustrates that it also has several child elements:

```
<!ELEMENT exception (icon?, display-name?, description?,
set-property*)>
```

Table 5 lists the exception element's attributes.

Table 5. The attributes of the exception element

Name	Description
className	The implementation class of the configuration bean that will hold the exception information. If specified, it must be a descendant of org.apache.struts.config.ExceptionConfig, which is the default class when no value is specified.
handler	The fully qualified Java class name of the exception handler that will process the exception. If no value is specified, the default class org.apache.struts.action.ExceptionHandler will be used. If a class is specified for this attribute, it must be a descendant of the ExceptionHandler class.
key	The message resources key specifying the error message associated with this exception.
path	The module-relative path of the resource to forward to if this exception occurs during the processing of an Action. This attribute is required.
scope	The identifier of the scope level where the ActionError instance should be stored. The attribute value must be either request or session. The default value is request.
type	The fully qualified Java class name of the exception that is to be handled. This attribute is required.
bundle	The servlet context attribute that identifies a resource bundle from which the key attribute of this element should come. If this attribute is not set, the default message resource for the current module is assumed.

The following example illustrates how to add an exception element at the global level:

```
<global-exceptions>
  <exception
    key="global.error.invalidlogin"
    path="/security/signin.jsp"
    scope="request"
    type="com.oreilly.struts.InvalidLoginException"/>
</global-exceptions>
```

The global-forwards Element

Every action finishes by forwarding or redirecting to a view. In most cases, this view is a JSP page or a static HTML page, but it can be another type of resource as well. Instead of referring to the view directly, the Struts framework uses the concept of a *forward* to associate a logical name to the resource. So, instead of referring to *login.jsp* directly, a Struts application might refer to this resource as the login forward.

The global-forwards section allows you to configure forwards that can be used by all actions within a module. The global-forwards section consists of zero or more forward elements:

```
<!ELEMENT global-forwards (forward*)>
```

The forward element maps a logical name to an application-relative URI. The application can then perform a forward or redirect using the logical name rather than the literal URI. This helps to decouple the controller and model logic from the view. The forward element can be defined in the global-forwards section as well as an action element. If a forward with the same name is defined in both places, the action level will take precedence.

The declaration of the forward element illustrates that it also has several child elements:

```
<!ELEMENT forward(icon?, display-name?, description,
set-property*)>
```

Table 6 lists the forward element's attributes.

Table 6. The attributes of the forward element

Name	Description
className	The implementation class of the configuration bean that will hold the forward information. The org.apache. struts.action.ActionForward is the default class when no value is specified.
contextRelative	Indicates whether the value of the path attribute should be considered context-relative if it starts with a slash (and is therefore not prefixed with the module prefix). The default value is false.
name	A unique value that is used to reference this forward in the application. This attribute is required.

Table 6. The attributes of the forward element (continued)

Name	Description
path	If the contextRelative attribute is true, the path is context-relative within the current web application (even if we are in a named module). If the contextRelative property is false, the path is the module-relative portion of the URL. This attribute is required and must begin with a slash (/) character.
redirect	A Boolean value that determines whether the RequestProcessor should perform a forward or a redirect when using this forward mapping. The default value is false, which means that a forward will be performed.

The following is an example of a global-forwards element:

```
<global-forwards>
  <forward name="Login" path="/security/signin.jsp"
    redirect="true"/>
  <forward name="SystemFailure"
    path="/common/systemerror.jsp"/>
  <forward
    name="SessionTimeOut"
    path="/common/sessiontimeout.jsp"
    redirect="true"/>
</global-forwards>
```

The action-mappings Element

The action-mappings element contains a set of action elements for a Struts application. The action-mappings element can contain zero or more action elements:

```
<!ELEMENT action-mappings (action*)>
```

The action element describes an ActionMapping object that is to be used to process a request for a specific module-relative URI. The action element also describes a mapping from a specific request path to a corresponding Action class. The controller selects a particular mapping by matching the URI path in the request with the path attribute in one of the action elements. The action element contains the following child elements:

```
<!ELEMENT action (icon?, display-name?, description,
set-property*, exception*, forward*)>
```

The attributes listed in Table 7 are available for the action element.

Table 7. The attributes of the action element

Name	Description
className	The implementation class of the configuration bean that will hold the action information. The org.apache.struts.action. ActionMapping class is the default class when no value is specified.
attribute	The name of the request or session scope attribute under which the form bean for this action can be accessed. A value is allowed here only if there is a form bean specified in the name attribute. This attribute has no default value. If both this attribute and the name attribute contain a value, this attribute will take precedence.
forward	A context-relative path of the web application resource that will process this request via RequestDispatcher.forward( ), instead of instantiating and calling the Action class. The attributes forward, include, and type are mutually exclusive.
include	A context-relative path of the web application resource that will process this request via RequestDispatcher.include( ), instead of instantiating and calling the Action class. The attributes forward, include, and type are mutually exclusive.
input	A context-relative path of the input form to which control should be returned if a validation error is encountered. This attribute is required if name is specified and the input bean returns validation errors.
name	The name of the form bean that is associated with this action. This value must be the name attribute from one of the form-bean elements defined earlier. This attribute has no default value.
path	A context-relative path of the submitted request, starting with a slash (/) character and omitting any filename extension if extension mapping is being used.
parameter	A general-purpose configuration parameter that can be used to pass extra information to the action instance selected by this action mapping. The Struts framework does not use this value in any way. If you provide a value here, you can obtain the value in your Action by calling the getParameter( ) method on the ActionMapping passed to the execute( ) method.

Table 7. The attributes of the action element (continued)

Name	Description
prefix	Used to match request parameter names to form bean property names. For example, if all of the properties in a form bean begin with "pre_", you can set the prefix attribute so the request parameters will match to the ActionForm properties. You can provide a value here only if the name attribute is specified.
roles	A comma-delimited list of security role names that are allowed to invoke this Action. When a request is processed, the RequestProcessor verifies the user has at least one of the roles identified within this attribute.
scope	Used to identify the scope within which the form bean is placed. It can be either request or session. It can be specified only if the name attribute is present. The default value is session.
suffix	Used to match request parameter names to form bean property names. For example, if all of the properties in a form bean end with "_foo", you can set the suffix attribute so the request parameters will match to the ActionForm properties. You can provide a value here only if the name attribute is specified.
type	A fully qualified Java class name that extends the org.apache.struts.action.Action class. It is used to process the request if the forward or include attributes are not specified. The attributes forward, include, and type are mutually exclusive.
unknown	A Boolean value indicating whether this action should be configured as the default for this application. If this attribute is set to true, this action will handle any request that is not handled by another action. Only one action mapping per application can have this value set to true. The default value is false.
validate	A Boolean value indicating whether the validate() method of the form bean, specified by the name attribute, should be called prior to calling the execute() method of this action. The default value is true.

The following is an example of an action element:

```
<action
  path="/signin"
  type="com.oreilly.strutssecurity.LoginAction"
  scope="request"
  name="loginForm"
  validate="true"
  input="/security/signin.jsp">
```

```
<forward
  name="Success"
  path="/index.jsp" redirect="true"/>
<forward
  name="Failure"
  path="/security/signin.jsp"
  redirect="true"/>
</action>
```

The controller Element

If you're familiar with Struts Version 1.0, you'll notice that
many of the parameters that were configured in the *web.xml*
for the controller servlet are now configured using the
controller element. Since the controller and its attributes are
defined in *struts-config.xml*, you can define a separate
controller element for each module. The declaration of the
controller element illustrates that it has a single child
element:

```
<!ELEMENT controller (set-property*)>
```

The controller element can contain zero or more set-
property elements and many different attributes, which are
listed in Table 8.

Table 8. The attributes for the controller element

Name	Description
className	The implementation class of the configuration bean that will hold the controller information. If specified, it must be a descendant of ControllerConfig, which is the default class when no value is specified.
bufferSize	The size of the input buffer used when processing file uploads. The default value is 4096.
contentType	The default content type and optional character encoding that are set for each response. The default value is text/ html. Even when a value is specified here, an action or a JSP page can override it.

Table 8. The attributes for the controller element (continued)

Name	Description
debug	The debugging level for this application. This value is used throughout the framework to determine how verbose the logging information should be for events that take place internally. The larger the value, the more verbose the logging is. This attribute is not required. The default value is 0, which causes little or no logging information to be written out. This attribute has been deprecated; you should now use your specific logging implementation to control the verbosity of log messages.

forwardPattern	A replacement pattern defining how the path attribute of a forward element is mapped to a context-relative URL when it starts with a slash (and when the contextRelative property is false). This value can consist of any combination of the following:
	$M
	    This is replaced by the module prefix of this module.
	$P
	    This is replaced by the path attribute of the selected forward element.
	$$
	    This causes a literal dollar sign to be rendered
	$x *(where x is any character not defined above)*
	    This is reserved for future use.
	If not specified, the default forwardPattern is MP, which is consistent with the previous behavior of forwards.

inputForward	Set to true if you want the input attribute of the action element to be the name of a local or global forward element. Set to false to treat the input attribute of action elements as a module-relative path.
locale	A Boolean value indicating whether the user's preferred Locale is stored in the user's session (if it is not already present). The default value is true.
maxFileSize	The maximum size (in bytes) of a file to be accepted as a file upload. This value can be expressed as a number followed by a K, M, or G, which is interpreted to mean kilobytes, megabytes, or gigabytes, respectively. The default value is 250M.

Table 8. The attributes for the controller element (continued)

Name	Description
memFileSize	The maximum size (in bytes) of a file whose contents will be retained in memory after uploading. Files larger than this threshold will be written to some alternative storage medium, typically a hard disk. This value can be expressed as a number followed by a K, M, or G, which is interpreted to mean kilobytes, megabytes, or gigabytes, respectively. The default value is 256K.
multipartClass	The fully qualified Java class name of the multipart request handler class to be used when uploading files from a user's local filesystem to the server. The default value is the org.apache.struts.upload. CommonsMultipartRequestHandler class.
nocache	A Boolean value indicating whether the framework should set nocache HTTP headers in every response. The default value is false.

pagePattern	A replacement pattern defining how the page attribute of custom tags is mapped to a context-relative URL of the corresponding resource. This value can consist of any combination of the following:
	$M
	    This is replaced by the module prefix of this module.
	$P
	    This is replaced by the path attribute of the selected forward element.
	$$
	    This causes a literal dollar sign to be rendered.
	$x *(where x is any character not defined above)*
	    This is reserved for future use.
	If not specified, the default pagePattern is MP, which is consistent with the previous behavior of URL calculation.

processorClass	The fully qualified Java class name of the request processor class to be used to process requests. The value specified here should be a descendant of RequestProcessor, which is the default value.
tempDir	Specifies the temporary working directory that is used when processing file uploads. This attribute is not required; the servlet container will assign a default value for each web application.

The `ControllerConfig` class is used to represent the information configured in the `controller` element in memory. The following fragment shows an example of how to configure the `controller` element:

```
<controller
 contentType="text/html;charset=UTF-8"
 debug="3"
 locale="true"
 nocache="true"
 processorClass=
 "com.oreilly.struts.CustomRequestProcessor"/>
```

The message-resources Element

The `message-resources` element specifies characteristics of the message resource bundles that contain the localized messages for an application. Each Struts configuration file can define one or more message resource bundles; therefore, each module can define its own bundles. The declaration of the `message-resources` element shows that it contains only a `set-property` element:

```
<!ELEMENT message-resources (set-property*)>
```

Table 9 lists the attributes for the `message-resources` element.

Table 9. The message-resources element's attributes

Name	Description
className	The implementation class of the configuration bean that will hold the message-resources information. If specified, it must be a descendant of MessageResourcesConfig, which is the default class when no value is specified.
factory	The fully qualified Java class name of the MessageResourcesFactory class that should be used. The class PropertyMessageResources is the default.
key	The servlet context attribute under which this message resources bundle will be stored. The default attribute is the value specified by the string constant at Globals. MESSAGES_KEY. The application module prefix (if any) is appended to the key (${key}${prefix}).

Table 9. The message-resources element's attributes (continued)

Name	Description
null	A Boolean value indicating how the MessageResources subclass should handle the case when an unknown message key is used. If this value is set to true, an empty string will be returned. If set to false, a message that looks something like "???global.label.missing???" will be returned. The actual message will contain the bad key. The default value is true.
parameter	This attribute is the base name of the resource bundle. For example, if the name of your resource bundle is *ApplicationResources.properties*, you should set the parameter value to ApplicationResources. This attribute is required. If your resource bundle is within a package, you must provide the fully qualified name in this attribute.

The following example shows how to configure multiple message-resources elements for a single application. Notice that the second element has to specify the key attribute, since there can be only one stored with the default key:

```
<message-resources
  null="false"
  parameter="StorefrontMessageResources"/>

<message-resources
  key="IMAGE_RESOURCE_KEY"
  null="false"
  parameter="StorefrontImageResources"/>
```

The plug-in Element

Plug-ins, a new feature to Struts, allow Struts applications to discover resources dynamically at startup. You must provide a nonabstract Java class that implements the org.apache. struts.action.PlugIn interface and add a plug-in element to the configuration file.

The plug-in element specifies a fully qualified class name of a general-purpose application plug-in module that receives notification of application startup and shutdown events. At startup, the framework will create an instance of each PlugIn class specified. The init( ) method is called when the application is started, and the destroy( ) method is called when the application is stopped.

The declaration of the plug-in element shows that it may contain zero or more set-property elements so that extra configuration information can be passed to your PlugIn class:

```
<!ELEMENT plug-in          (set-property*)>
```

There is a single attribute for the plug-in element, which is listed in Table 10.

Table 10. The attribute for the plug-in element

Name	Description
className	The fully qualified Java class name of the plug-in class. It must implement the PlugIn interface.

The following fragment shows two plug-in elements being used:

```
<plug-in
  className=
  "com.cavaness.banking.service.memory.MemoryDatabasePlugIn">

  <set-property property="pathname"
    value="/WEB-INF/database.xml"/>
</plug-in>

<plug-in
  className="org.apache.struts.validator.ValidatorPlugIn">
  <set-property
    property="pathnames" value=
    "/WEB-INF/validator-rules.xml,/WEB-INF/validation.xml"/>
</plug-in>
```

PART II

Using Struts ActionForms

What Are ActionForms?

The Jakarta Struts framework provides the `org.apache.struts.action.ActionForm` class, which can be used to persist the HTML form data in memory long enough for it to be validated. Once all validation problems are resolved, the data within the `ActionForm` objects can be used to transfer the form data into the application for processing.

ActionForms and Scope

`ActionForm` objects can be configured to have two different levels of scope: `request` and `session`. If *request scope* is used, an `ActionForm` will be available only until the end of the request/response cycle. Once the response has been returned to the client, the `ActionForm` and the data within it are no longer accessible.

If you need to keep the form data around for more than a single request, you can configure an `ActionForm` to have *session scope*. This might be necessary if your application captures data across multiple pages, similar to a wizard dialog. Unless you specifically need to hold the form data across multiple requests, you should use request scope for your `ActionForm` objects. The `scope` attribute within the `action` element is used to specify the scope of the `ActionForm`:

```
<action
    path="/viewsignin"
```

```
    parameter="/signin.jsp"
    type="org.apache.struts.actions.ForwardAction"
    scope="request"
    name="loginForm"
    validate="false"
    input="/index.jsp">
</action>
```

The scope attribute applies to the ActionForm specified by the name attribute in the action element. If the action doesn't require an ActionForm, you can leave out the scope attribute. If you don't specify a scope attribute for an action mapping, the ActionForm will default to session scope.

The Life Cycle of an ActionForm

When an ActionForm detects one or more validation errors, it performs a forward to the resource identified in the input attribute. The data that was sent in the request is left in the ActionForm so that it can be used to repopulate the HTML fields. This process is shown in Figure 1.

The framework will attempt to reuse ActionForm objects when available. This behavior reduces the number of short-lived objects created within the JVM and helps to reduce the garbage collection cycles.

Creating an ActionForm

There are only three real differences between the ActionForms for any application:

- The properties that the ActionForm defines
- The validate( ) method
- The reset( ) method

The ActionForm class provided by the Struts framework is abstract, and so you will need to create subclasses (or use DynaActionForm, which is discussed later) in order to capture your application-specific form data. Within your subclass,

---

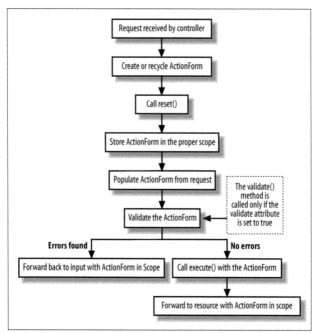

Figure 1. The life cycle of an ActionForm

you should define a property for each field that you wish to capture from the HTML form. For example, suppose we want to capture the username and password fields from a form. The following ActionForm class illustrates an example called LoginForm that can be used to store and validate the username and password fields:

```
public class LoginForm extends ActionForm {

  private String password = null;
  private String username = null;

  public void setUsername(String username) {
    this.username = username;
  }
```

```java
  public String getUsername() {
    return (this.username);
  }

  public String getPassword() {
    return (this.password);
  }

  public void setPassword(String password) {
    this.password = password;
  }

  public ActionErrors validate(ActionMapping mapping,
                               HttpServletRequest request)
  {

    ActionErrors errors = new ActionErrors();

    // Get access to the message resources
    // for this application
    MessageResources resources =
      (MessageResources)request.getAttribute(
        Action.MESSAGES_KEY );

    if(getUsername() == null ||
      getUsername().length() < 1) {
    String usernameLabel =
      resources.getMessage( "label.username" );

      errors.add( ActionErrors.GLOBAL_ERROR,
                  new ActionError("errors.required",
                    usernameLabel ));
    }

    if(getPassword() == null ||
      getPassword().length() < 1) {
    String passwordLabel =
      resources.getMessage( "label.password" );
      errors.add( ActionErrors.GLOBAL_ERROR,
                  new ActionError("errors.required",
                    passwordLabel ));
    }
    return errors;
  }
}
```

When an HTML form is submitted, an instance of the LoginForm listed will be created and populated from the request parameters. The framework does this by matching each request parameter name against the corresponding property name in the ActionForm class.

The validate( ) Method

The ActionForm class contains a validate( ) method that can be called by the RequestProcessor. Whether it's called depends on two things. First, an ActionForm must be configured for an action mapping. This means that the name attribute for an action element must correspond to the name attribute of one of the form-bean elements in the configuration file.

The second condition that must be met before the RequestProcessor will invoke the validate( ) method is that the validate attribute in the action mapping must have a value of true. The following shows an action element that uses the LoginForm and meets both requirements:

```
<action
    path="/signin"
    type="com.oreilly.struts.storefront.security.LoginAction"
    scope="request"
    name="loginForm"
    validate="true"
    input="/security/signin.jsp">

    <forward
      name="Success"
      path="/index.jsp"
      redirect="true"/>
</action>
```

When the *signin* action is invoked, the framework will populate an instance of a LoginForm using the values it finds in the request. Since the validate attribute has a value of true, the validate( ) method in the LoginForm will be called.

The ActionForm reset( ) Method

The ActionForm class also supports a reset( ) method. As the ActionForm life cycle diagram (Figure 1) illustrated, the reset( ) method is called for each new request, regardless of the scope of the ActionForm, before the ActionForm is populated from the request.

The reset( ) method in the base ActionForm contains no default behavior, since no properties are defined in this abstract class. Applications that extend the ActionForm class are allowed to override this method and reset the ActionForm properties to whatever state they wish. This can include setting boolean properties to true or false, setting string values to null or some initialized value, or even instantiating instances of other objects that the ActionForm holds onto. For an ActionForm that has been configured with request scope, the framework will create a new instance for each new request; therefore, there's not much need to reset( ) the values back to any default state. ActionForms that are configured with session scope are different, however, and this is when the reset( ) method comes in handy.

Declaring ActionForms in the Struts Configuration File

Once you have created a class that extends ActionForm, you need to configure the class in the Struts configuration file. The first step is to add a new form-bean element to the form-beans section of the file:

```
<form-beans>
  <form-bean
    name="loginForm"
    type=
      "com.oreilly.struts.storefront.security.LoginForm"/>
</form-beans>
```

The value for the type attribute must be the fully qualified
Java class name of ActionForm.

Once you have defined your form-bean, you can now use it in
one or more action elements. It's very common to share one
ActionForm across several actions. To use an ActionForm in an
action element, you must specify a few attributes for each
action mapping that uses the ActionForm. These attributes are
name, scope, and validate:

```
<action
  path="/signin"
  input="/security/signin.jsp"
  name="loginForm"
  scope="request"
  type="com.oreilly.struts.storefront.security.LoginAction"
  validate="true">
  <forward name="Success" path="/index.jsp"
    redirect="true"/>
</action>
```

The Struts framework will instantiate an instance of the
ActionForm specified in the name attribute and automatically
populate it from the request.

Using an ActionForm

Once you have configured the ActionForm for a particular
Action, you can then insert and retrieve its values within the
execute( ) method, as the following example illustrates:

```
public ActionForward execute( ActionMapping mapping,
      ActionForm form,
      HttpServletRequest request,
      HttpServletResponse response )
  throws Exception{
```

```
// Get the user's login name and password. They should
// have already been validated by the ActionForm.
String username = ((LoginForm)form).getUsername();
String password = ((LoginForm)form).getPassword();

// Login through the security service
Beer4AllService serviceImpl =
  this.getBeer4AllService();

// Attempt to authenticate the user
UserView  userView =
  serviceImpl.authenticate(username, password);

UserContainer existingContainer =
     getUserContainer(request);
existingContainer.setUserView( userView );

return mapping.findForward(Constants.SUCCESS_KEY);
  }
}
```

As this example demonstrates, the properties of the
ActionForm can be accessed and used to pass back to other
parts of the application. Notice, however, that although the
ActionForm is passed in to the execute( ) method, it's the type
of the ActionForm abstract superclass. You will need to
explicitly cast it to the proper type in order to access your
properties:

```
String username = ((LoginForm)form).getUsername();
String password = ((LoginForm)form).getPassword();
```

The DynaActionForm Class

Using the ActionForm class has many advantages over manu-
ally performing similar functionality. Since the behavior that
the ActionForm class provides is needed in nearly every web
application, using the framework to perform the work can
greatly reduce development time. Having stated the benefits
of using the ActionForm class, there are a few very important
downsides to using them.

The first and foremost problem with using ActionForms is the sheer number of classes that it can add to a project. Even if you share ActionForm definitions across many pages, the additional classes make it more difficult to manage a project. Another major liability is the requirement to define the properties in the ActionForm that must be captured from the HTML form. If a property is added or removed from the HTML form, the ActionForm class may need to be modified and recompiled.

For these reasons, a new type of ActionForm was added to the framework—it is dynamic in nature and allows you to avoid creating concrete ActionForm classes for your application. The dynamic ActionForm is implemented by the base class org.apache.struts.action.DynaActionForm, which extends the ActionForm class.

The validation of the data for a DynaActionForm is a little more complicated than a standard ActionForm. This is because the Struts Validator framework must be used rather than coding the validate( ) method. However, using the Validator framework is much more powerful and flexible. The combination of using dynamic ActionForms with the Validation framework could make using standard ActionForms obsolete.

Configuring Dynamic ActionForms

To use the DynaActionForm in your Struts application, you first need to add a form-bean element to the configuration file, just as with regular ActionForms.

The difference between configuring a regular ActionForm and a DynaActionForm is that you must include one or more form-property elements in order for the dynamic form to have properties. An example of configuring a DynaActionForm in the Struts configuration file is shown here:

```
<form-beans>
  <form-bean
    name="loginForm"
    type="org.apache.struts.action.DynaActionForm">
```

```
<!-- Specify the dynamic properties of the form -->
<form-property
  name="username"
  type="java.lang.String"/>
<form-property
  name="password"
  type="java.lang.String"/>

<!-- You can also set the initial value
     of a property -->
<form-property
  initial="false"
  name="rememberMe"
  type="java.lang.Boolean"/>
  </form-bean>
<form-beans>
```

The properties are what make this ActionForm dynamic. At
runtime, the framework creates an instance of the
DynaActionForm class and makes it possible to set and get the
configured property values. To add new properties, you only
need to modify the configuration file. No source code needs
to be changed, and you no longer need to create concrete
ActionForm classes. The power and flexibility that this provides is immense.

The form-property element also allows you to specify the initial value for each property. The framework will set the property to that value when the application is started. The initial
value is also used when the reset( ) method is called to reset
the values back to their original state.

If you don't include the initial attribute, then properties
will be assigned default values based on the Java programming language; numbers to zero and properties of type
Object will be assigned a null value.

NOTE

The type attribute expects a fully qualified Java class
name. Therefore, you must use the wrapper classes for
primitives.

DynaActionForm and Validation

The DynaActionForm doesn't provide any default behavior for the validate() method. Unless you subclass the DynaActionForm class and override the validate() method, there's no easy way to validate using the DynaActionForm. Fortunately, the framework comes to your aid again with the Struts Validator.

The DynaValidatorForm can be used with the Validator to declaratively configure which dynamic ActionForms and their associated properties are validated. In order to use the Validator, perform the following steps:

1. Choose which validation rules your dynamic ActionForms use in *validation.xml*.

2. Tell your application that it will be using the Validator framework.

Creating the validation.xml File

The Validator framework is shipped with many of the most common validation rules that an application might require. The first step is to configure which of the rules your application needs and for which ActionForm. You must create an XML file (commonly named *validation.xml*) that describes which dynamic ActionForm uses which of the validation rules. The name of the dynamic ActionForm that was configured in the form-bean element must be specified. In the following example, we set the name attribute to the same value that was specified in the earlier example:

```
<form-validation>
 <global>
 </global>
 <formset>
  <form name="loginForm">
    <field
      property="username"
      depends="required">
```

```
      <arg0 key="label.username"/>
    </field>
    <field
      property="password"
      depends="required ">
      <arg0 key="label.password"/>
    </field>
  </form>
</formset>
</form-validation>
```

This XML configuration is all that's needed to set up the proper dynamic validation routines.

Plugging in the Validator

To configure a Struts application to use the Validator framework, you must take advantage of another new feature of the 1.1 release: the Struts PlugIn mechanism. In the Struts configuration file, add the following XML:

```
<plug-in className=
  "org.apache.struts.validator.ValidatorPlugIn">
  <set-property
    property="pathnames"
    value="/WEB-INF/validator-rules.xml,
      /WEB-INF/validation.xml"/>
</plug-in>
```

The value attribute specifies the *validation-rules.xml* file (which you should not need to modify) and the *validation. xml* file (which you create). If you choose another name for the *validation.xml* file or separate your application's validation rules into separate files, you will need to alter the value attribute shown here.

PART III

Built-in Action Classes

A Struts Action class extends the controller component to bridge a client request with a business operation. You will typically implement an Action class for each business operation, or group of related operations, in your application. Struts includes five out-of-the-box Action classes in the org.apache.struts.actions package (listed in Table 11), which you can use directly, or subclass and expand, to save yourself development time.

Table 11. The built-in Action classes

Action class	Description
DispatchAction	Supports related operations in a single Action class
ForwardAction	Forwards to a non-Struts component implemented as a servlet or JSP
IncludeAction	Includes response content from a non-Struts component implemented as a servlet or JSP
LookupDispatchAction	Dispatches a request based on a reverse lookup of a request parameter value in the resource bundle
SwitchAction	Switches from one application module to another and forwards control to a resource in the second module

DispatchAction

The DispatchAction allows multiple operations to reside in a single class instead of being scattered throughout multiple

Action classes. For example, instead of creating separate `AddItemAction` and `UpdateShoppingCartAction` classes for a *ShoppingCart* service, you could combine this functionality into a single class that implements a method to support each requirement.

To use the `DispatchAction`, create a class that extends it, and implement a method for each function that you need to perform on the service. Your class should not contain the typical `execute()` method as other `Action` classes do; the `execute()` method is implemented by the abstract `DispatchAction`. In your subclass, you instead implement multiple methods that accept the same parameters as `execute()` but have names that correspond to the operations.

The following is an example structure a `DispatchAction` subclass might take:

```
package com.oreilly.struts.storefront.order;
// imports omitted

public class ShoppingCartActions extends DispatchAction {

  public ActionForward addItem(ActionMapping mapping,
    ActionForm form, HttpServletRequest request,
    HttpServletResponse response) throws Exception {

    // Call the service layer to perform the operation
    // (details omitted)

    return mapping.findForward(IConstants.SUCCESS_KEY);
  }

  public ActionForward update(ActionMapping mapping,
    ActionForm form, HttpServletRequest request,
    HttpServletResponse response) throws Exception {

    // Call the service layer to perform the operation
    // (details omitted)

    return mapping.findForward(IConstants.SUCCESS_KEY);
  }
}
```

In this example, the `addItem()` and `update()` methods support the required operations. The following entry illustrates how the `ShoppingCartActions` class is declared in the Struts configuration file:

```
<action path="/cart"
  input="/order/shoppingcart.jsp"
  parameter="method"
  scope="request"
  type=
  "com.oreilly.struts.storefront.order.ShoppingCartActions"
  validate="false">
  <forward name="Success" path="/order/shoppingcart.jsp"
    redirect="true"/>
</action>
```

The */cart* action mapping specifies the `parameter` attribute and sets the value to be the literal string `"method"`. The `DispatchAction` uses this attribute value to determine which method in your subclass to invoke. When a call is made to the action mapping */cart*, an additional request parameter must be passed where the key is the value specified for the `parameter` attribute. The value of this request parameter must be the exact name of the method to invoke. For example, to invoke the `addItem()` method, you would refer to the action like this:

```
<html:form action="cart?method=addItem">
```

ForwardAction

There may be situations where you need to access servlets or JSPs from your applications that are not integrated into the Struts framework. You could just forward from one JSP page to another without going through an `Action` class, but this prevents the controller from performing its role within an MVC application.

Rather than making a direct call to the component, you should map your request to an `Action` class that performs a simple forward to the desired resource. Unless you need to do something special in addition to the forward, ForwardAction provides this behavior for you. This Action simply performs a forward to a URI that is configured for it. You specify an action element for a ForwardAction as shown in the following:

```
<action
  input="/index.jsp"
  path="/viewsignin"
  parameter="/security/signin.jsp"
  type="org.apache.struts.actions.ForwardAction">
</action>
```

When the */viewsignin* path is selected, the execute( ) method of the ForwardAction class is called. The parameter attribute of the action element defines the destination of the forward.

The following example shows how to configure a ForwardAction for a servlet call:

```
<action
  input="/index.jsp"
  path="/downloadFile"
  parameter="/myDownloadServlet"
  type="org.apache.struts.actions.ForwardAction">
</action>
```

For this example, */myDownloadServlet* must correspond to the url-pattern for a servlet-mapping entry in your *web.xml* file.

NOTE

You can also define a simple forward by specifying the forward attribute in an action mapping instead of type.

IncludeAction

The IncludeAction is similar to the ForwardAction in that its purpose is to make it easier to integrate existing JSP and servlet-based components into a Struts-based application. The difference is that this action includes the output of a resource in the response instead of forwarding to that resource. To accomplish this, the execute( ) method of the IncludeAction builds a RequestDispatcher based on the path to a resource and then executes an include( ) on that dispatcher.

The following action mapping configures an IncludeAction:

```
<action
  path="/checkStatus"
  parameter="/statusServlet"
  type="org.apache.struts.actions.IncludeAction">
</action>
```

You must include the parameter attribute and specify a path to the resource that you wish to include.

NOTE

You can also define a simple include by specifying the include attribute in an action mapping instead of type.

LookupDispatchAction

The LookupDispatchAction is a subclass of DispatchAction intended to make it easier to support HTML forms with multiple submit buttons having the same name. For example, one submit button may be tied to a "Checkout" action, and another to a "Save Order" action. Both buttons would have the same name—for example, "action"—but the value of each button would be different.

Just like the DispatchAction, the LookupDispatchAction allows you to specify a class with multiple methods, where one of the methods is invoked based on the value of a special request parameter that is identified in your configuration file. The DispatchAction uses the value of the request parameter directly to determine which method to invoke; however, the LookupDispatchAction uses the value of the request parameter to perform a reverse lookup from the resource bundle. It is the message key from the bundle entry matching the parameter value that determines the method called in this case. When supporting multiple buttons in an HTML form, the parameter value of interest is the value of the button that was pressed.

Create a class that extends LookupDispatchAction, and implement the getKeyMethodMap( ) method. This method returns a Map. Each key in this Map must match a key in the resource bundle. For each key, the corresponding value in the Map is the name of the method that should be invoked when the request parameter equals the message string found in the resource bundle for that key. The following is an example getKeyMethodMap( ) method implementation:

```
protected Map getKeyMethodMap( ) {
  Map map = new HashMap( );
  map.put("button.checkout", "checkout" );
  map.put("button.saveorder", "saveorder" );
  return map;
}
```

Define the following message resource bundle entries:

```
button.checkout=Checkout
button.saveorder=Save Order
```

Define the following action element for the LookupDispatchAction subclass:

```
<action path="/processcheckout"
  input="/checkout.jsp"
  name="checkoutForm"
  parameter="action"
  scope="request"
  type="com.oreilly.struts.storefront.order.
    ProcessCheckoutAction">
  <forward name="Success" path="/order/ordercomplete.jsp"/>
</action>
```

The value of the parameter attribute in the action element defines the request parameter of interest. The following JSP fragment defines the two submit buttons for the example:

```
<html:form action="/processcheckout">
  <html:submit property="action">
    <bean:message key="button.checkout"/>
```

```
    </html:submit>
    <html:submit property="action">
      <bean:message key="button.saveorder"/>
    </html:submit>
  </html:form>
```

Depending on which button is pressed, submission of the form will include a request parameter named "action" with a value of either "Checkout" or "Save Order". The ProcessCheckoutAction will take the received value and find the corresponding message resource key in the bundle, either button.checkout or button.saveorder. The mapping returned by getKeyMethodMap( ) then defines the method to call based on this key.

SwitchAction

The SwitchAction supports switching from one application module to another, and then forwarding control to a resource within the target module. The following *struts-config.xml* file entry declares a mapping for a SwitchAction:

```
<action path="/switch"
  type="org.apache.struts.actions.SwitchAction"/>
```

WARNING

Use of application modules requires the use of extension mapping.

There are two required request parameters when using a SwitchAction. The prefix parameter specifies the application prefix, beginning with a /, of the application module to which control should be switched. If you need to switch to the default module, use a zero-length string.

The second required parameter is the page parameter. This parameter should specify the application-relative URI, beginning with a /, to which control should be forwarded once the correct application module is selected.

The link created by the following example switches from the default module to reference a viewOrder action declared in a module named order:

```
<html:link action="switch?prefix=/order&page=/viewOrder.do">
  Switch to View Order
</html:link>
```

You could accomplish the same behavior with a forward to either of the following global forward declarations:

```
<forward name="goToViewOrder" contextRelative="true"
  path="/order/viewOrder.do"/>
<forward name="switchToViewOrder"
  path="/switch.do?prefix=/order&amp;page=/viewOrder.do"/>
```

PART IV

Tag Reference

The Struts custom tag libraries allow you to interact with the rest of the framework without including Java code in your JSP pages. For example, the following line illustrates how to use a tag to render the value of a JavaBean property within a table cell without the use of a scriptlet:

```
<td>Hello <bean:write name="user" property="firstName"/>
</td>
```

In this example, bean identifies the tag library, write is the tag name, and name and property are both tag attributes. The attributes used here identify the bean to access and the particular property to render.

The Struts tags are organized into the Bean, HTML, Logic, Nested, and Tiles libraries. The following sections define the tags in each library and describe how to use them. The Struts distribution also includes the Template tag library, but these tags have been deprecated in favor of Tiles.

Conventions

The following conventions apply to the tag attribute descriptions in this reference:

- An attribute is optional unless explicitly noted as required.

- An attribute can be assigned a value using a runtime expression (a scriptlet) unless noted otherwise.

Common Tag Attributes

Tag behavior is determined by the attribute values you supply. The individual tag descriptions that follow this section define the attributes by tag. To minimize repetition, several attributes that are used consistently across many tags are defined up front in Table 12.

Table 12. Common tag attributes

Attribute	Description
bundle	The name of the application scope bean under which the MessageResources object is stored. Defaults to Globals.MESSAGES_KEY.
id	Names the scripting variable created by the tag, as well as the key value used to locate the bean in the scope defined by the scope attribute.
locale	The name of the session scope bean under which the currently selected Locale object is stored. Defaults to Globals.LOCALE_KEY.
name	The key value used to look up an existing bean in the scope defined by the scope attribute.
property	Identifies the JavaBeans property (of the bean identified by name) whose value is used by the tag. If not specified, the bean identified by name is itself used as the value.
scope	Identifies the JSP scope ("page", "request", "session", or "application") within which a particular bean will be searched for (using the name attribute) or created (under the key value given by the id attribute). If not specified, searches for existing beans follow the order listed above, and new beans are created in page scope.

The previous example of the bean:write tag illustrated how to access a bean property using the name and property attributes. In the following example, a bean (a simple String) is created using the id and scope attributes of the bean:define tag and then output by the bean:write tag using its name:

```
<!-- Create a new String as a bean under the key
     "myNewBean" -->
<bean:define id="myNewBean" scope="page" value="MyValue"/>
```

```
<!-- Retrieve myNewBean as a value to write -->
<bean:write name="myNewBean" scope="page"/>
```

Using JavaBeans with Struts Tags

JavaBeans play a major role in the use of the Struts tags.
These JavaBeans may be ActionForms, where each property of
the ActionForm corresponds to an input field in the HTML
form. In other cases, the beans may simply be value objects
from the model layer. These beans can be in any scope: page,
request, session, or application. You most often use bean
properties when working with a tag that has a property
attribute.

Accessing Simple Properties

Consider a simple property reference within a tag, such as:

```
property="firstName"
```

This is converted to a method call on the corresponding
bean. Based on standard JavaBeans naming conventions, this
example property would be accessed using getFirstName( )
or setFirstName(String) methods. Struts uses the Java intro-
spection APIs to identify the names of the actual property
getter and setter methods, so your beans can also provide
customized method names through the use of a BeanInfo
class.

Accessing Nested Properties

Nested references are used to access a property through a
hierarchy of property names separated by periods (.). For
example, consider the following property reference:

```
property="user.address.city"
```

This reference is translated into the Java expression:

```
getUser( ).getAddress( ).getCity( )
```

If a nested reference is used in a setter, the property setter is called on the last property in the chain. For the above property reference, the equivalent expression would be:

```
getUser().getAddress().setCity("Dallas")
```

Accessing Indexed Properties

Subscripts can be used to access individual elements of a property whose value is an array, a List, or whose underlying JavaBean offers indexed getter and setter methods. For example, when indexed getter and setter methods are present, you might have the following property reference:

```
property="address[2]"
```

This reference is translated into the Java expression:

```
getAddress(2)
```

The same property reference in a setter would call:

```
setAddress(2, address)
```

Bean Tags

The Struts Bean tag library provides access to JavaBeans and their associated properties, as well as defining new beans that are accessible to the remainder of the page via scripting variables and scoped attributes. The Bean tags are listed in Table 13.

Table 13. The Bean tag library

Tag name	Description
cookie	Define a scripting variable based on the value(s) of a request cookie.
define	Define a scripting variable based on the tag body content, a bean property, or a specified value.
header	Define a scripting variable based on the value(s) of a request header.

Table 13. The Bean tag library (continued)

Tag name	Description
include	Load the response from a dynamic application request and make it available as a bean.
message	Render an internationalized message string.
page	Expose an object from the page context as a bean.
parameter	Define a scripting variable based on the value(s) of a request parameter.
resource	Load a web application resource and make it available as a bean.
size	Create an Integer bean that holds the number of elements in a Collection or Map.
struts	Expose a named Struts internal configuration object as a bean.
write	Render the value of a bean or bean property.

cookie

Retrieve a cookie value (or values) from the request and create a corresponding page scope attribute of type javax. servlet.http.Cookie (or Cookie[]). The cookie tag's attributes are listed in Table 14.

Table 14. The cookie tag's attributes

Attribute	Description
id	See the Common Tag Attributes. (Required.)
multiple	Assign any non-null value to create a Cookie[] result. If not specified, the first (or only) value of the cookie is exposed as a Cookie.
name	The case-sensitive name of the request cookie. (Required.)
value	The default value to return if the named cookie is not present in the request.

define

Create a scripting variable and a bean under a specified scope with a value given in one of three ways:

- Specify a name (and optionally a property and/or scope) to retrieve the value from another bean. The new attribute's type will match that of the retrieved value unless it is a primitive. In this case, the corresponding wrapper class is used.
- Assign a String using the value attribute.
- Assign a String by supplying a nonempty tag body.

Don't specify both name and value (or either of these attributes with a nonempty tag body), or an exception will be thrown.

The define tag's attributes are listed in Table 15.

Table 15. The define tag's attributes

Attribute	Description
id name property scope	See the Common Tag Attributes. id is required; property and scope apply only if name is specified.
toScope	The scope of the created bean. Defaults to page scope.
type	The fully qualified class name applied to the created scripting variable. Applies only when name is used to copy a bean or bean property. Defaults to java.lang.Object.
value	Use this attribute to create a bean of type String with the specified value.

The Common Tag Attributes were illustrated using the value attribute to define a bean. The following code demonstrates the other two approaches:

```
<!-- Create a String using the tag body content -->
<bean:define id="bodyString">Use this text</bean:define>

<!-- Copy an existing bean -->
<bean:define id="userCopy" name="user"
 type=
 "com.oreilly.struts.storefront.customer.view.UserView"/>
```

header

Retrieve a header value (or values) from the request and create a corresponding page scope attribute of type String (or String[]). The header tag's attributes are listed in Table 16.

Table 16. The header tag's attributes

Attribute	Description
id	See the Common Tag Attributes. (Required.)
multiple	Assign any non-null value to create a String[] result. If not specified, the first (or only) value of the header is exposed as a String.
name	The case-insensitive name of the request header. (Required.)
value	The default value to return if the named header is not present in the request.

The following example demonstrates retrieving a header value with a default value specified:

```
<!-- Display the language header value -->
<bean:header id="languageValue" name="accept-language"
  value="en-us"/>
<bean:write name="languageValue"/>
```

include

Perform an internal dispatch to the specified application component or external URL, and expose the response data as a page scope bean of type String. The name used to access this String is defined by the id attribute. You must specify exactly one of the forward, href, or page attributes for use in generating the URL. If you specify forward or page and the current request is part of a session, the generated request will also include the session identifier. The include tag's attributes are listed in Table 17.

Table 17. The include tag's attributes

Attribute	Description
anchor	Specify an anchor tag (without the "#") to be added to the generated hyperlink.
forward	The name of a global ActionForward.
href	Absolute URL (including the protocol prefix, such as http:) of the resource to be included.
id	See the Common Tag Attributes. (Required.)
page	Application-relative URI (starting with a "/") of the resource to be included.
transaction	Set to true to include the current transaction control token in the generated URL.

Here is an example using an absolute URL:

```
<!-- Retrieve the contents of a DTD as a String -->
<bean:include id="dtdContents"
 href="http://jakarta.apache.org/struts/dtds/
   struts-config_1_1.dtd"/>
```

message

Render an internationalized message based on a message key and locale. You can supply up to five parametric replacements for the message. The message key can be specified directly using the key attribute, or indirectly using the name and property attributes to obtain it from a bean. A value obtained from a bean must be a String. The message tag's attributes are listed in Table 18.

Table 18. The message tag's attributes

Attribute	Description
arg0	First parametric replacement value.
arg1	Second parametric replacement value.
arg2	Third parametric replacement value.
arg3	Fourth parametric replacement value.
arg4	Fifth parametric replacement value.

Table 18. The message tag's attributes (continued)

Attribute	Description
bundle locale name property scope	See the Common Tag Attributes. If key is not specified, the bean property identified by these attributes is used as the message key.
key	The message key. If not specified, the key is obtained from a bean using name, property, and scope.

The following is an example of the message tag:

```
<!-- Retrieve the user's first name from a bean -->
<!-- and display an internationalized message   -->
<bean:define id="userName" name="user" property="firstName"
 type="java.lang.String"/>
<bean:message key="welcome.message" arg0="<%=userName%>"/>
```

where a corresponding resource bundle entry might be:

```
welcome.message=Welcome {0}!
```

page

Expose the ServletContext, ServletConfig, ServletRequest, ServletResponse, or HttpSession from the page context as a scripting variable and page scope bean. The page tag's attributes are listed in Table 19.

Table 19. The page tag's attributes

Attribute	Description
id	See the Common Tag Attributes. (Required.)
property	Name of the page context property to be retrieved and exposed. Must be one of application, config, request, response, or session. (Required.)

parameter

Retrieve a parameter value (or values) and create a page scope attribute of type String (or String[]). Depending on the multiple attribute, either getParameter() or getParameterValues() is called on the request object. The parameter tag's attributes are listed in Table 20.

Table 20. The parameter tag's attributes

Attribute	Description
id	See the Common Tag Attributes. (Required.)
multiple	Assign any non-null value to create a String[ ] result. If not specified, the first (or only) value of the parameter is exposed as a String.
name	The case-sensitive name of the request parameter. (Required.)
value	The default value to return if the named parameter is not present in the request.

resource

Retrieve the value of the specified web application resource, and make it available as either an InputStream or a String. If the input attribute is specified, an InputStream will be created. Otherwise, the resource will be read into a String. The resource tag's attributes are listed in Table 21.

Table 21. The resource tag's attributes

Attribute	Description
id	See the Common Tag Attributes. (Required.)
input	Assign any non-null value to create an InputStream instead of a String.
name	Application-relative name (starting with a "/") of the web application resource to be loaded and made available. (Required.)

Here is an example that opens an InputStream on the web application's configuration file:

```
<bean:resource id="stream" name="/WEB-INF/web.xml"
  input="true"/>
```

size

Create a page scope Integer bean whose value represents the number of elements held in an array, Collection, or Map. Either the collection or name attribute must be specified. An exception is thrown if the retrieved object is null or not of one of the required types. The size tag's attributes are listed in Table 22.

Table 22. The size tag's attributes

Attribute	Description
collection	A runtime expression that evaluates to an array, a Collection, or a Map.
id	See the Common Tag Attributes. (Required.)
name property scope	See the Common Tag Attributes. If specified, these attributes must identify a bean or property of one of the required types.

struts

Expose a Struts internal configuration object as a page scope bean and scripting variable. Specify exactly one of the following attributes: formBean, forward, or mapping. The created bean will be a FormBeanConfig, ForwardConfig, or ActionConfig object. The struts tag's attributes are listed in Table 23.

Table 23. The struts tag's attributes

Attribute	Description
id	See the Common Tag Attributes. (Required.)
formBean	The name of an ActionFormBean.
forward	The name of a global ActionForward.
mapping	The matching path of an ActionMapping.

Here is an example of accessing an ActionConfig object:

```
<!-- Check the validate property of an ActionMapping -->
<bean:struts id="signinConfig" mapping="/signin"/>
<bean:write name="signinConfig" property="validate"/>
```

write

Render the value of a bean or bean property. If the value is a String, it is rendered unchanged. If the value is a Number or Date, the format can be specified by the format attribute, or looked up in a resource bundle using a formatKey or a default Struts key. For all other types, toString() is called on the value object and that result is rendered unchanged. The write tag's attributes are listed in Table 24.

Table 24. The write tag's attributes

Attribute	Description
bundle locale name property scope	See the Common Tag Attributes. At a minimum, name is required to identify the value to render.
filter	Set this attribute to true to replace characters in the result that are sensitive in HTML. Defaults to true.
format	A format string for rendering a Number or Date.
formatKey	A key used to locate the format string in the application resources. Used for a Number or Date if format is not specified.
ignore	Set this Boolean attribute to true to do nothing if the specified bean does not exist (instead of throwing an exception). Defaults to false.

The following is a simple example of using the write tag to display the value of a bean property:

```
<bean:write name="user" property="firstName"/>
```

The following is an example using the format attribute:

```
<%
  // create some test beans
  Date currentDate = new Date();
  request.setAttribute("currentDate", currentDate);
  Double dbl = new Double(-1.2345);
  request.setAttribute("dbl", dbl);
%>
```

```
<table>
<!-- Display a Date with and without a format string -->
<tr><td><bean:write name="currentDate"/></td></tr>
<tr><td><bean:write name="currentDate"
        format="EEEE, MMMM dd, yyyy"/></td></tr>

<!-- Display a Double with and without a format string -->
<tr><td><bean:write name="dbl"/></td></tr>
<tr><td><bean:write name="dbl" format="#.##;(#.##)"/></td>
</tr>
</table>
```

which produces output like the following:

```
Mon Feb 17 13:17:10 EST 2003
Monday, February 17, 2003
-1.2345
(1.23)
```

The format attribute illustrates how patterns are applied, but rather than using this attribute, you should typically define your patterns in resource bundles and use the formatKey attribute to apply them by locale. For example, you could define the following resource bundle entry for use with the write tag:

```
number.format=#.##;(#.##)
```

This format could then be referenced using the formatKey attribute:

```
<bean:write name="dbl" formatKey="number.format"/>
```

NOTE

Refer to the java.text.DecimalFormat and java.text.SimpleDateFormat JavaDocs for guidelines on defining format strings.

HTML Tags

The Struts HTML tag library contains tags that help create HTML input forms, as well as other tags that are generally useful in the creation of HTML-based user interfaces. These tags (listed in Table 25) are designed to work very closely with the other components of the Struts framework.

Table 25. The HTML tag library

Tag name	Description
base	Renders a `<base>` element
button	Renders a button input field
cancel	Renders a cancel button
checkbox	Renders a checkbox input field
errors	Conditionally renders a set of error messages
file	Renders a file select input field
form	Renders a `<form>` element
frame	Renders a `<frame>` element
hidden	Renders a hidden field
html	Renders an `<html>` element
image	Renders an input tag of type image
img	Renders an HTML img tag
javascript	Renders JavaScript validation based on the validation rules loaded by the `ValidatorPlugIn`
link	Renders an HTML anchor or hyperlink
messages	Conditionally displays a set of accumulated messages
multibox	Renders multiple checkbox input fields
option	Renders a select option
options	Renders a collection of select options
optionsCollection	Renders a collection of select options
password	Renders a password input field
radio	Renders a radio button input field
reset	Renders a reset button input field
rewrite	Renders a URI
select	Renders a `select` element
submit	Renders a submit button

Table 25. The HTML tag library (continued)

Tag name	Description
text	Renders an input field of type text
textarea	Renders an input field of type textarea

Common HTML Attributes

Several attributes related to basic HTML functionality, keyboard navigation, and stylesheets are common to many of the tags in this library. These attributes are described in Table 26, and the individual tag descriptions indicate which tags support them.

Table 26. Common attributes for the HTML tags

Attribute	Description
accesskey	The keyboard character used to move focus immediately to this element.
alt	The alternate text for this element.
altKey	The message resources key for this element's alternate text.
disabled	Set to true to disable an input field.
indexed	Valid only inside of a logic:iterate tag. Set to true to include the current value of an iteration counter as part of the HTML tag name. The counter value will be rendered inside brackets ([ ]).
style	The CSS styles to be applied to the HTML element.
styleClass	The CSS stylesheet class to be applied to the HTML element (includes a class attribute for the tag).
styleId	The identifier to be assigned to this HTML element (includes an id attribute).
tabindex	The tab order (ascending positive integers) for this element.
title	The advisory title for this element.
titleKey	The message resources key for this element's advisory title.

With the exception of indexed, these attributes correspond to standard HTML functionality. The following example illustrates the use of the indexed attribute. The details of the iterate tag shown here are covered in the Logic Tags section.

```
<%
  // create a test collection
  List myCollection = new ArrayList( );
  myCollection.add("Entry 1");
  myCollection.add("Entry 2");
  request.setAttribute("myCollection", myCollection);
%>

<logic:iterate id="entry" name="myCollection"
  type="java.lang.String">
  <html:text name="controlName" property="propertyName"
    indexed="true"
    value="<%=entry%>"/>
</logic:iterate>
```

This code produces the following HTML output:

```
<input type="text" name="controlName[0].propertyName"
  value="Entry 1">
<input type="text" name="controlName[1].propertyName"
  value="Entry 2">
```

JavaScript Event Handlers

Many of the HTML tags allow you to specify JavaScript event handlers. For example, to configure an *onClick* handler for a supported tag, you can assign the JavaScript function name to the onclick attribute for the tag. Table 27 lists the attributes for the supported event handlers.

Table 27. JavaScript event handler attributes

Attribute	Description
onblur	Executed when this element loses input focus
onchange	Executed when this element loses input focus and its value has changed
onclick	Executed when this element receives a mouse click
ondblclick	Executed when this element receives a mouse double-click
onfocus	Executed when this element receives input focus

Table 27. JavaScript event handler attributes (continued)

Attribute	Description
onkeydown	Executed when this element has focus and a key is depressed
onkeypress	Executed when this element has focus and a key is depressed and released
onkeyup	Executed when this element has focus and a key is released
onmousedown	Executed when this element is under the mouse pointer and a mouse button is depressed
onmousemove	Executed when this element is under the mouse pointer and the pointer is moved
onmouseout	Executed when this element was under the mouse pointer, but the pointer is then moved outside the element
onmouseover	Executed when this element was not under the mouse pointer, but the pointer is then moved inside the element
onmouseup	Executed when this element is under the mouse pointer and a mouse button is released

HTML Tag Descriptions

In the tag description tables that follow, a "Common attributes" entry is included if the tag supports all or most of the Common HTML Attributes and JavaScript Event Handlers. If only a few of the common attributes are supported, those attributes are instead listed individually.

base

Render an HTML base element that identifies the absolute location of the enclosing JSP page. This ensures that any relative URL references within the page are resolved based on the page's actual location, and not on the URL to which the most recent submit took place. You should include this tag in your JSPs as a matter of habit to support relative URLs, such as those for images. The base tag must be placed within the HTML <head> element. Its attributes are listed in Table 28.

Table 28. The base tag's attributes

Attribute	Description
server	Specify a server name to use in place of the name held in the request.
target	The window target for relative URLs in the page. For example, specifying "_blank" for this standard HTML attribute causes hyperlinks in the page defined using relative URLs to open a new window when selected.

The following is the most common usage of the base tag:

```
<head>
  <html:base/>
</head>
```

For a web server running on your local machine, this example would produce output of the form:

```
<head>
  <base href="http://localhost:8080/storefront/index.jsp">
</head>
```

button

Render an HTML input element of type button. The button label is defined by a specified value or the content of the tag body. This tag is valid only when nested inside an <html:form> tag body. Its attributes are listed in Table 29.

Table 29. The button tag's attributes

Attribute	Description
Common attributes	See the Common HTML Attributes and JavaScript Event Handlers.
property	The name assigned to the generated input field. (Required.)
value	Specify the button label to display. Defaults to the tag body (if present), or "Click" otherwise.

cancel

Render an HTML input element of type submit. The button label is defined by a specified value or the content of the tag body. This tag is valid only when nested inside an <html:form> tag body. Its attributes are listed in Table 30.

The button produced by the cancel tag is unique in that the validate() method for the form is skipped when it is pressed. The RequestProcessor bypasses any validation and just calls the execute() method for the form's action.

Table 30. The cancel tag's attributes

Attribute	Description
Common attributes	See the Common HTML Attributes and JavaScript Event Handlers.
property	The name of the request parameter that will be included with this submission. Do not set this attribute unless you need to do your own detection of a cancel. The Struts controller will not recognize this button as a cancel if any name other than the internally assigned default is used.
value	Specify the button label to display. This value will also be submitted as the value of the specified request parameter. Defaults to the tag body (if present), or "Cancel" otherwise.

checkbox

Render an HTML input element of type checkbox. The checked status is determined by a property of the form bean (or another bean identified by the name attribute). This tag is valid only when nested inside an <html:form> tag body. Its attributes are listed in Table 31.

The underlying property value associated with this field should be of type boolean, and any value you specify should correspond to one of the case-insensitive strings that indicate a true value ("true", "yes", or "on").

The browser will only send values in the request for the checkboxes that are checked. In order to correctly recognize unchecked checkboxes, the ActionForm bean associated with this form must include a statement setting the corresponding Boolean property to false in the reset() method.

Table 31. The checkbox tag's attributes

Attribute	Description
Common attributes	See the Common HTML Attributes and JavaScript Event Handlers.
name	The bean whose properties are consulted when rendering the current value of this input field. Defaults to the enclosing form bean if not specified.
property	The name of the bean property associated with the field and the request parameter included when the form is submitted. (Required.)
value	The value to be transmitted if this checkbox is checked when the form is submitted. Defaults to "on".

Typical usage of the checkbox element is as follows:

```
<!-- Associate a boolean form property with a checkbox -->
<html:checkbox property="myBooleanProperty"/>
```

errors

Render one or more error messages stored in the request. The messages supported by this tag are typically created either in the validate( ) method of an ActionForm or by the exception handling framework. Error messages can be stored using an ActionErrors object, a String, or a String[]. This tag renders nothing if no error messages are present.

You can standardize your error message displays through a set of bundle entries with the following keys:

errors.header
: Text rendered before the message list

errors.prefix
: Text rendered before each error message

errors.suffix
: Text rendered after each error message

errors.footer
: Text rendered after the message list

For example, you can display a bulleted list of errors with a header message by setting these bundle entries to:

```
errors.header=
<h3><font color="red">Validation Error</font></h3>
You must correct the following error(s) before
proceeding:<ul>
errors.footer=</ul><hr>
errors.prefix=<li>
errors.suffix=</li>
```

The property attribute gives you additional flexibility in displaying errors. When an error message is added to the request, it can be associated with a property string. If, for example, this string corresponded to the name of the bean property that an error applies to, you could group error messages by field, or only display those relating to a particular field. Table 32 contains a full list of the errors tag's attributes.

Table 32. The errors tag's attributes

Attribute	Description
bundle locale	See the Common Tag Attributes.
name	The name of the request scope bean under which the error messages have been stored. Defaults to Globals.ERROR_KEY.
property	The name of the property for which error messages should be displayed. If not specified, all error messages are displayed.

For a basic error display using the resource bundle header and footer, all that is required is the following:

```
<html:errors/>
```

file

Render an HTML input element of type file. To support a file upload, the enclosing form must be configured as method="POST" and enctype="multipart/form-data". However, this tag is better suited for use with an ActionForm when simply assigning a file name to a String property, as opposed to performing a file upload. This tag is valid only when nested inside an `<html:form>` tag body. Its attributes are listed in Table 33.

Table 33. The file tag's attributes

Attribute	Description
Common attributes	See the Common HTML Attributes and JavaScript Event Handlers.
accept	Comma-delimited set of MIME types to which the selected file should be limited. Most browsers ignore this HTML attribute.
maxlength	Maximum number of input characters to accept. Defaults to no limit. Most browsers ignore this HTML attribute.
name	The bean whose properties are consulted when rendering the current value of this input field (if value is not specified). Defaults to the enclosing form bean if not specified.
property	Name of the bean property associated with the field (if value is not specified) and the request parameter included when the form is submitted. (Required.)
size	Approximate size (in characters) of the file name box to be displayed.
value	Assign a specific value to the corresponding HTML tag attribute.

NOTE

Although this tag renders the value attribute within the file input control it creates, this attribute has little meaning. For security reasons, most browsers ignore this initial value when displaying the file name box or setting the default location for the file browse dialog. This value is also typically ignored if the form is submitted without a user selection being made.

---

form

Render an HTML form tag and link that form with an ActionForm. When an HTML field name and an ActionForm property name match, the property from the ActionForm is used to populate the HTML field. When the HTML form is submitted, the framework stores the user's input in the ActionForm. The form tag's attributes are listed in Table 34.

Table 34. The form tag's attributes

Attribute	Description
action	The URL to which this form will be submitted. The ActionForm and its scope are identified based on the ActionMapping identified here. If extension mapping is being used (*.do), this value should equal the path attribute of the action, optionally followed by the extension suffix. If path mapping is being used, this value should equal the exact path attribute of the action. (Required.)
enctype	The content encoding used to submit a form (when method is set to POST).
focus	The field name to which initial focus will be assigned for this page.
focusIndex	If the focus field is a field array, such as a radio button group, use this attribute to specify the array element that receives focus.
method	The HTTP method (either GET or POST) that will be used to submit this request. Defaults to POST.
onreset	The JavaScript event handler executed if the form is reset.
onsubmit	The JavaScript event handler executed if the form is submitted.
style styleClass styleId	See the Common HTML Tag Attributes.
target	The frame target to which this form is submitted.

Here is a form example that references several common tags in the Bean and HTML libraries:

```
<html:form action="login" focus="username">
  <table>
    <tr>
      <th><bean:message key="label.username"/></th>
    </tr>
    <tr>
      <td>
        <!-- Text input box for entering the username -->
        <html:text property="username" size="20"
          maxlength="20"/>
```

```
        <!-- Display error messages
            stored for this property -->
        <html:errors property="username"/>
      </td>
    </tr>
    <tr>
      <th><bean:message key="label.password"/></th>
    </tr>
    <tr>
      <td>
        <!-- Password input box for
            entering the password -->
        <html:password property="password" size="20"
          maxlength="16"
          redisplay="false"/>
        <!-- Display error messages stored for this
            property -->
        <html:errors property="password"/>
      </td>
    </tr>
    <tr>
      <td>
        <!-- Submit button with a
            label from the bundle -->
        <html:submit><bean:message key="label.login"/>
          </html:submit>
      </td>
    </tr>
  </table>
</html:form>
```

frame

Render an HTML <frame> element. The content for a frame
is determined using attributes (listed in Table 35) that paral-
lel those of the link tag. You must specify exactly one of the
action, forward, href, or page attributes for calculation of the
base URL for the frame source. Refer to the description of
the link tag to see how to append parameters to the generated URL using the tag attributes.

Table 35. The frame tag's attributes

Attribute	Description
action forward href page	Refer to the link tag description for an explanation of how to use these attributes to define the URL for the frame content source.
anchor	Specify an anchor tag (without the "#") to be added to the generated hyperlink.
frameborder	Specify "yes" or "1" for this attribute to display a border around the frame.
frameName	Value for the name attribute of the rendered <frame> element.
longdesc	URI of a long description of the frame. This is a supplement for the title aimed at nonvisual user agents.
marginheight	The amount of space (in pixels) between the frame's contents and its top and bottom margins.
marginwidth	The amount of space (in pixels) between the frame's contents and its left and right margins.
name paramId paramName paramProperty paramScope property scope	Refer to the link tag description for an explanation of how to use these attributes to append parameters to the frame content URL.
noresize	Set to true to disallow users from resizing the frame.
scrolling	Indicate whether scroll bars should be created unconditionally (yes), never (no), or only when needed (auto).
style styleClass styleId title titleKey	See the Common HTML Attributes.
transaction	Set to true to include the current transaction control token in the generated hyperlink.

hidden

Render an HTML <input> element of type hidden, defaulting to the specified value or the specified property of the bean associated with the current form. This tag is valid only when nested inside an <html:form> tag body. Its attributes are listed in Table 36.

Table 36. The hidden tag's attributes

Attribute	Description
Common attributes	According to the TLD, this tag supports most of the Common HTML Attributes and JavaScript Event Handlers. However, few of these attributes apply in practice because a hidden field can never gain focus, lose focus, accept user input, etc.
name	The bean whose properties are consulted when rendering the current value of this input field. Defaults to the enclosing form bean if not specified.
property	The name of this input field, and the name of the corresponding bean property if value is not specified. (Required.)
value	The value to which this field should be initialized. Defaults to the corresponding bean property value.
write	Specify true to render the field value onto the page in addition to the HTML element. Defaults to false.

html

Render an html element and optionally output language attributes for the user's locale. Table 37 lists the html tag's attributes.

Table 37. The html tag's attributes

Attribute	Description
locale	Set to true to record a Locale based on the current request's Accept-Language header (if any) if none is currently set. Defaults to false.
xhtml	Set to true to render an xml:lang attribute on the generated html element. This also causes all other tags from this library to render as XHTML. Defaults to false.

image

Render an HTML input element of type image. The base URL for the image is calculated either directly (based on the value specified in the src or page attributes) or indirectly (by looking up a message resource string based on the srcKey or pageKey attributes). You must specify exactly one of these four attributes. This tag is valid only when nested inside an <html:form> tag body. Its attributes are listed in Table 38.

Pressing an image button performs a form submit. When this occurs, two parameters are included in the request to represent the x and y coordinates of the mouse click on the image. Given a property value of MyImage, these parameters would be named MyImage.x and MyImage.y. If you do not specify a property, a blank string will be used by default and the parameters will be passed simply as x and y. You can define x and y as properties in your form to have these values automatically mapped when the form is submitted.

Table 38. The image tag's attributes

Attribute	Description
Common attributes	See the Common HTML Attributes and JavaScript Event Handlers.
align	Deprecated HTML attribute for image alignment; replaced by CSS.
border	The width (in pixels) of the border around this image.
bundle locale	See the Common Tag Attributes.
page	The module-relative path (starting with "/") of the image.
pageKey	The resource bundle key for the module-relative path of the image.
property	The value for the name attribute in the HTML tag. Defaults to an empty string.
src	The absolute URL of the image.
srcKey	The resource bundle key for the image URL.
value	The value for the value attribute in the HTML tag.

img

Render an HTML <img> element. The base URL for the image is calculated either directly (based on the value specified in the src or page attributes) or indirectly (by looking up a message resource string based on the srcKey or pageKey attributes). You must specify exactly one of these four attributes. Table 39 contains a full list of the img tag's attributes.

Refer to the description of the link tag to see how to append parameters to the generated URL using the supported tag attributes. Although the URL here refers specifically to an image, the approach is identical to the one used to build a URL for a hyperlink.

Table 39. The img tag's attributes

Attribute	Description
Common attributes	See the Common HTML Attributes and JavaScript Event Handlers. The following attributes do not apply to this tag: acesskey, disabled, indexed, tabindex, onblur, onchange, and onfocus.
align	Deprecated HTML attribute for image alignment; replaced by CSS.
border	The width of the border (in pixels) surrounding the image.
bundle locale	See the Common Tag Attributes.
height	Specify the image height (in pixels), if known, to improve page rendering performance.
hspace	Specify the horizontal spacing (in pixels) between the image and any text to the left or right.
imageName	Provide a value for a name attribute to be included in the rendered HTML element.
ismap	If a server-side image map is being used, specify the name of that map.

Table 39. The img tag's attributes (continued)

Attribute	Description
name paramId paramName paramProperty paramScope property scope	Refer to the `link` tag description for an explanation of how to use these attributes to append parameters to the image URL.
page pageKey src srcKey	Refer to the `image` tag description for an explanation of how to use these attributes to define the image URL.
usemap	If a client-side image map is being used, specify the name of the map defined within this page (prefixed with "#") that defines the hot-spot areas of the image.
vspace	Specify the vertical spacing (in pixels) between the image and any text above or below.
width	Specify the image width (in pixels), if known, to improve page rendering performance.

Here is an `img` tag example:

```
<html:img page="/multimedia/mufflers.gif" align="top"
  border="2" hspace="10" imageName="mufflerImage"/>
```

javascript

Render JavaScript validation methods based on the validation rules loaded by the `ValidatorPlugIn`. Use the attributes listed in Table 40 to control which methods are generated. Set `staticJavascript` to `true` to include the general methods, such as `validateRequired(form)` and `validateMaxLength(form)`. Set `dynamicJavascript` to `true` and define the `formName` to include form-specific code that calls the static methods and defines the field-specific error messages. You can use this control over which method types are rendered to generate the static methods in a single page so that they can be cached by the browser.

If you take this approach, you only need to generate the dynamic methods in your other pages.

Table 40. The javascript tag's attributes

Attribute	Description
cdata	If XHTML has been enabled, specify true (the default) to wrap the JavaScript in a CDATA section to prevent XML parsing.
dynamicJavascript	Specify true (the default) to render the dynamic JavaScript. (Runtime expression not allowed.)
formName	Specify a form name to render specific rules and error messages.
htmlComment	If not in XHTML mode, specify true (the default) to enclose the rendered JavaScript within HTML comments.
method	Specify an alternate method name for the main validation method. The default is the form name prefixed with validate.
page	The current page of a set of validation rules if the page attribute for the XML file's field element is in use.
src	Define the HTML src attribute for the <script> element if you need to include an external script.
staticJavascript	Specify true (the default) to render the static JavaScript. (Runtime expression not allowed.)

The following line renders both the static and dynamic validation methods needed by the named form:

```
<html:javascript formName="userDetailForm/>
```

link

Render an HTML <a> element as an anchor definition (if linkName is specified) or as a hyperlink to a specified URL. Define the text to display for a hyperlink using the tag body.

Specify exactly one of the action, forward, href, or page attributes for calculation of the base URL for the hyperlink. You can dynamically append parameters to this URL using either one or both of the following approaches:

- Identify a bean or bean property using `paramName` either alone or in conjunction with `paramProperty`. You can optionally scope the bean name using `paramScope`. The value (converted to a `String` if necessary) is appended as a request parameter with the name given by `paramId`.

- Identify a bean or bean property that holds a `Map` of parameter names and values using `name` either alone or in conjunction with `property`. You can optionally scope the bean name using `scope`. Value objects other than strings and string arrays are converted using `toString( )`. Multiple values are passed for a parameter if a `String[ ]` is held in the `Map`.

Table 41 lists the `link` tag's attributes.

Table 41. The link tag's attributes

Attribute	Description
Common attributes	See the Common HTML Attributes and JavaScript Event Handlers. The following attributes do not apply to this tag: `alt`, `altKey`, `disabled`, `tabindex`, and `onchange`.
action	Logical name of an `ActionMapping` that contains the content-relative URI of the hyperlink. Ignored if `linkName` is specified.
anchor	Specify an anchor tag (without the "#") to be added to the hyperlink.
forward	Logical name of a global `ActionForward` that contains the content-relative URI of the hyperlink. Ignored if `linkName` is specified.
href	Absolute URL (including the protocol prefix, such as `http:`) for the hyperlink. Ignored if `linkName` is specified.
indexId	Override the parameter name used to store the current index when this `link` tag is inside a `logic:iterate` tag. Defaults to `"index"`.
linkName	Provide a value for a name attribute to be included in the rendered HTML anchor tag. The HTML tag will not include an `href` if this attribute is specified.
name	The name of a bean that either is a `Map` of query parameters itself or has a property (identified by the `property` attribute) that holds the desired `Map`. Ignored if `linkName` is specified.

Table 41. The link tag's attributes (continued)

Attribute	Description
page	The module-relative path (beginning with a "/" character) of the hyperlink. Ignored if `linkName` is specified.
paramId	The name of the request parameter that will be appended to the frame source URL if `paramName` is specified. Ignored if `linkName` is specified.
paramName	The name of a bean that either is a parameter value itself or has a property (identified by the `paramProperty` attribute) that holds the desired value. Ignored if `linkName` is specified.
paramProperty	Use this attribute to retrieve a parameter value from a property of the bean identified by `paramName`. Ignored if `linkName` is specified.
paramScope	The scope within which to search for the bean specified by `paramName`. If not specified, all scopes are searched. Ignored if `linkName` is specified.
property	Use to retrieve a `Map` of parameter values from a property of the bean identified by `name`. Ignored if `linkName` is specified.
scope	The scope within which to search for the bean specified by `name`. If not specified, all scopes are searched. Ignored if `linkName` is specified.
target	Optionally specify a window target, such as "_self" or a frame name, in which the resource requested by this hyperlink will be displayed.
transaction	Set to `true` to include any current transaction control token in the generated hyperlink.

messages

Iterate over a collection of general-purpose or error messages stored in the request. Messages can be stored using an `ActionMessages` object, an `ActionErrors` object, a `String`, or a `String[]`. The iteration is simply skipped if no messages are present.

This tag is similar to the errors tag, but it offers more flexibility. By providing only an iterator, the messages tag gives you more control over how the messages are displayed. Its attributes are listed in Table 42.

Table 42. The messages tag's attributes

Attribute	Description
bundle locale	See the Common Tag Attributes.
footer	Specify a message resource key to identify a footer to display after the message iteration has finished.
header	Specify a message resource key to identify a header to display before the message iteration begins.
id	Provide a name for the page scope bean created by the tag to represent the current message in the iteration. (Required.)
message	Set this attribute to true to retrieve messages from the request using Globals.MESSAGE_KEY as the key. If this attribute is set to true, the name attribute is ignored. Defaults to null if not specified.
name	Identify the request scope bean under which the messages have been stored. Defaults to Globals.ERROR_KEY.
property	Name of the property for which messages should be displayed. If not specified, all messages are displayed.

This example of the messages tag:

```
<% // Generate some test messages (usually done by an
   // Action class instead of here in the JSP)
  ActionMessages messageHolder = new ActionMessages();
  messageHolder.add(ActionMessages.GLOBAL_MESSAGE,
    new ActionMessage("order.submitted"));
  messageHolder.add(ActionMessages.GLOBAL_MESSAGE,
    new ActionMessage("order.onBackorder", "3"));
  request.setAttribute(Globals.MESSAGE_KEY, messageHolder);
%>

<ul>
<html:messages id="message" message="true"
 header="order.header" footer="order.footer">
  <li><bean:write name="message"/></li>
  <br>
</html:messages>
</ul>
```

using these bundle entries:

```
order.header=Order Status
order.footer=Thank you for your business!
order.submitted=Your order has been submitted.
order.onBackorder={0} item(s) are on backorder.
```

renders the following HTML:

```
<ul>
Order Status
  <li>Your order has been submitted.</li>
  <br>

  <li>3 item(s) are on backorder.</li>
  <br>
Thank you for your business!
</ul>
```

multibox

Render an HTML input element of type checkbox, whose "checked" status is initialized based on whether the specified value matches one of the elements of an array of current values. This tag is useful when you need to support multiple selections from a related set of choices. The associated form property should be a String[] that holds the selections made, and each checkbox should represent an available choice. This tag is valid only when nested inside an <html: form> tag body. Its attributes are listed in Table 43.

To correctly recognize the case where none of the associated checkboxes has been selected, you must set the selected value array to a zero length array in the reset( ) method of the form.

Table 43. The multibox tag's attributes

Attribute	Description
Common attributes	See the Common HTML Attributes and JavaScript Event Handlers. indexed is not supported by this tag.
name	The bean whose properties are consulted when rendering the current value of this input field. Defaults to the enclosing form bean if not specified.

Table 43. The multibox tag's attributes (continued)

Attribute	Description
property	Name of the String[ ] bean property associated with the field and the request parameter name included when the form is submitted. (Required.)
value	The value to be transmitted if this checkbox is checked when the form is submitted. If not specified, the tag body content is used.

Here is an example using a list of items selected by an item number:

```
<!-- Iterate through the available item choices -->
<logic:iterate id="item" name="catalogForm"
  property="itemChoices">

  <!-- Display a text label for this choice -->
  <bean:write name="item" property="displayLabel"/>

  <!-- The form holds a String[] of
       selected item numbers -->
  <html:multibox property="selectedItemNumbers">

    <!-- Write the item number for this choice as
         the multibox tag body. This value will be
         compared to the selectedItemNumbers array
         to check the box or not. -->
    <bean:write name="item" value="itemNumber"/>

  </html:multibox>
</logic:iterate>
```

option

Render an HTML <option> element representing one of the choices for an enclosing <select> element. The text displayed to the user comes from the body of this tag or from a message string that is looked up based on the bundle, locale, and key attributes. This tag can appear multiple times within a select tag and can be used in conjunction with options and optionsCollection.

If the value of the corresponding bean property matches the specified value, this option will be marked as selected. This tag is valid only when nested inside an <html:select> tag body. Its attributes are listed in Table 44.

Table 44. The option tag's attributes

Attribute	Description
bundle locale	See the Common Tag Attributes.
disabled	Set to true if this option should be disabled.
key	Defines the message key to be used to look up the text displayed for this option. If not specified, the display text is taken from the tag's body content.
style styleClass styleId	See the Common HTML Attributes.
value	Value to be submitted for this field if the user selects this option. (Required.)

Here is an example using the option tag to display choices retrieved from a resource bundle:

```
<html:select property="contactMethod" size="1">
  <html:option key="label.email" value="email"/>
  <html:option key="label.phone" value="phone"/>
</html:select>
```

options

Render a set of HTML <option> elements representing possible choices for an enclosing <select> element. This tag can appear multiple times within a select tag and can be used in conjunction with option and optionsCollection. Its attributes are listed in Table 45.

If the collection attribute is specified, the tag operates as follows:

- The collection attribute is interpreted as the name of a bean in some scope that represents a collection of individual beans, one per option value to be rendered.

- The `property` attribute is interpreted as the name of a property of the individual beans in the collection and is used to retrieve the values assigned to the options.

- The `labelProperty` attribute is interpreted as the name of a property of the individual beans in the collection and is used to retrieve the labels displayed for the options. If not specified, the property named by the `property` attribute determines both the displayed label and the value for each option.

If the `collection` attribute is not specified, the tag operates as follows:

- If only `name` is specified, the attribute identifies a bean in some scope that is the collection of option values.

- If only `property` is specified, the attribute identifies a property of the associated form bean that holds the collection of option values.

- If both `name` and `property` are specified, the specified property of the named bean holds the collection of option values.

- If neither `labelName` nor `labelProperty` is specified, the option labels are the same as the option values.

- If only `labelName` is specified, the attribute identifies a bean in some scope that is the collection of option labels.

- If only `labelProperty` is specified, the attribute identifies a property of the associated form bean that holds the collection of option labels.

- If both `labelName` and `labelProperty` are specified, the specified property of the named bean holds the collection of option labels.

When the `collection` attribute is not specified, note that `toString()` is applied directly to the elements in the collections to retrieve the values and labels. These collection elements are not treated as beans with properties designated for these purposes.

Table 45. The options tag's attributes

Attribute	Description
collection	Name of a bean in some scope that is the collection of options. The property and labelProperty attributes are used to define the values and display labels.
filter	Set to true to filter characters in the option labels that are sensitive in HTML. Defaults to true.
labelName	Name of a bean in some scope that contains the collection of option display labels.
labelProperty	Property of the form bean or the bean specified by the labelName attribute that holds the collection of option display labels.
name	Name of a bean in some scope that contains the collection of options. Defaults to the form bean if collection is not specified.
property	Property of the form bean or the bean specified by the name attribute that holds the collection of options.
style styleClass	See the Common HTML Attributes.

In the following example, separate collections are specified for the option values and labels:

```
<html:select property="defaultAddress">
  <html:options name="addressChoiceValues"
    labelName="addressChoiceLabels"/>
</html:select>
```

Refer to the description of the select tag for an example of using the collection attribute of the options tag.

optionsCollection

Render a set of HTML <option> elements representing possible choices for an enclosing <select> element. This tag can appear multiple times within a select tag and can be used in conjunction with option and options. Its attributes are listed in Table 46.

The individual options are built from a collection of beans identified either by the name attribute alone, or by name and property. The `label` and `value` attributes identify the bean properties used to define the option labels and values. This tag is similar to the `options` tag, but it uses the `name` and `property` attributes more consistently and simplifies obtaining the collection from the form bean.

Table 46. The optionsCollection tag's attributes

Attribute	Description
filter	Set to `true` to filter characters in the option labels that are sensitive in HTML. Defaults to `true`.
label	The property of the bean within the collection that defines the option label. Defaults to "label".
name	The bean whose properties are consulted when rendering the current value of this input field. Defaults to the enclosing form bean if not specified.
property	The property of the form bean or the bean specified by the name attribute that holds the collection of options. (Required.)
style styleClass	See the Common HTML Attributes.
value	The property of the bean within the collection that defines the option value. Defaults to "value".

Here is an example using both `option` and `optionsCollection`:

```
<html:select property="defaultAddress" size="1">
  <html:option key="label.noSelection" value=""/>
  <html:optionsCollection property="addresses"
   value="addressId"
   label="addressName"/>
</html:select>
```

In this example, a collection is obtained from the `addresses` property of the form bean. For each object in the collection, the `addressId` and `addressName` properties are retrieved to define the option value and label.

password

Render an HTML `input` element of type `password`, defaulting to the specified `value` or the specified `property` of the form.

This tag is valid only when nested inside an <html:form> tag body. Its attributes are listed in Table 47.

Table 47. The password tag's attributes

Attribute	Description
Common attributes	See the Common HTML Attributes and JavaScript Event Handlers.
maxlength	Maximum number of input characters to accept. Defaults to no limit.
name	The bean whose properties are consulted when rendering the current value of this input field. Defaults to the enclosing form bean if not specified.
property	Name of the request parameter that will be included with this submission. It is also the bean property used for initialization if value is not specified. (Required.)
readonly	Set to true if this input field should be read-only.
redisplay	Set to false to prevent an existing value from being rendered in the HTML element. Even though asterisks will be shown on the visible HTML page, the actual password value will be visible in the HTML source for the page. Defaults to true.
size	Approximate size (in characters) of the input box to be displayed.
value	Specify an initial value for the field.

You'll typically use a password tag with redisplay set to false:

```
<html:password property="password" size="12" maxlength="10"
 redisplay="false"/>
```

radio

Render an HTML input element of type radio. A comparison between the field's assigned value and the current value for the associated bean property determines the checked status of the field. The name and property attributes always determine the current value used in this comparison. However, you have two options for specifying a particular radio field's value. If a logic:iterate tag is being used to build a group of radio choices, use the radio tag's idName attribute to associate the field to the current bean in the iteration. Then use the value attribute to define the name of the property that is to be retrieved from the iteration bean and assigned as the radio field value. If the `radio` tag is not being used within an iteration, define the value attribute directly. This tag is valid only when nested inside an `<html:form>` tag body. Its attributes are listed in Table 48.

Table 48. The radio tag's attributes

Attribute	Description
Common attributes	See the Common HTML Attributes and JavaScript Event Handlers.
idName	Name of the bean exposed by an `iterate` tag that holds the value for the `radio` tag. Use the value attribute to specify the bean property.
name	The bean whose properties are consulted when rendering the checked status of this field. Defaults to the enclosing form bean if not specified.
property	The bean property that holds the current selection from the group of options associated with this `radio` tag. (Required.)
value	The property name to retrieve from the bean identified by idName or an explicit value for the `radio` tag. (Required.)

Here is an example with radio values specified directly:

```
<html:radio property="selectedItemNumber" value="123"/>
Item Number 123
<html:radio property="selectedItemNumber" value="456"/>
Item Number 456
```

The following is an example with radio values defined by a bean property in an iteration:

```
<!-- Iterate through the available
     item choices held in the form -->
<logic:iterate id="item" name="catalogForm"
  property="itemChoices">

  <!-- Use the itemNumber property from the iterate
       bean as the radio value. The radio button will
       be checked if the value matches the form's
       selectedItemNumber property. -->
  <html:radio idName="item" property="selectedItemNumber"
   value="itemNumber"/>
```

```
<!-- Display a label for this radio choice -->
<bean:write name="item" property="displayLabel"/>
</logic:iterate>
```

reset

Render an HTML input element of type reset. The button label is defined by a specified value or the content of the tag body. The reset tag's attributes are listed in Table 49.

Table 49. The reset tag's attributes

Attribute	Description
Common attributes	See the Common HTML Attributes and JavaScript Event Handlers.
property	Name assigned to the generated input field.
value	Value of the label to be placed on this button. Defaults to the tag body (if present) or "Reset" otherwise.

rewrite

Render a request URI in the same manner as the link tag without creating the <a> hyperlink. This tag is useful when you want to generate a URL string for use by another tag, an HTML element, or a JavaScript method.

Specify exactly one of the action, forward, href, or page attributes for calculation of the base URL. Refer to the description of the link tag to see how to append parameters to the generated URL using the tag attributes. Table 50 lists the rewrite tag's attributes.

Table 50. The rewrite tag's attributes

Attribute	Description
action forward href page	Refer to the link tag description for an explanation of how to use these attributes to define the URL.
anchor	Specify an anchor tag (without the "#") to be added to the hyperlink.

Table 50. The rewrite tag's attributes (continued)

Attribute	Description
name paramId paramName paramProperty paramScope property scope	Refer to the link tag description for an explanation of how to use these attributes to append parameters to the URL.
transaction	Set to true to include any current transaction control token in the generated hyperlink.

In the following example, a rewrite is used to define the URL to an external JavaScript:

```
<SCRIPT language='javascript'
 src='<html:rewrite page="/scripts/common.js"/>'>
</SCRIPT>
```

select

Render an HTML select element associated with a specified bean property. If multiple is specified, this property must correspond to an array type. This tag is valid only when nested inside an <html:form> tag body. Its attributes are listed in Table 51.

To correctly recognize cases where no selection is made, the ActionForm must reset the corresponding property to a default value (if multiple is not set) or a zero-length array (if multiple is set) in its reset() method.

Table 51. The select tag's attributes

Attribute	Description
Common attributes	See the Common HTML Attributes and JavaScript Event Handlers.
multiple	Set to any non-null value if the rendered <select> element should support multiple selections.
name	The bean whose properties are consulted to determine which option should be preselected when rendering this field. Defaults to the enclosing form bean if not specified.

Table 51. The select tag's attributes (continued)

Attribute	Description
property	Name of the bean property that determines the initial selection (if value is not specified) and the request parameter included when the form is submitted. (Required.)
size	The number of available options displayed at one time.
value	The value to compare with for marking an option as selected (overrides the current value of the form property).

The following is an example of a select tag and its options:

```
<!-- The countryCode form property holds the selection -->
<html:select property="countryCode">
  <!-- The countryList collection is another bean
       (not accessed through the form) that defines
       the choices -->
  <html:options collection="countryList" property="code"
   labelProperty="description" />
</html:select>
```

submit

Render an HTML input element of type submit. The button label is defined by a specified value or the content of the tag body. The submit tag's attributes are listed in Table 52.

Table 52. The submit tag's attributes

Attribute	Description
Common attributes	See the Common HTML Attributes and JavaScript Event Handlers.
property	Name of the request parameter that will be included with this submission, set to the specified value.
value	Specify the button label to display. This value will also be submitted as the value of the specified request parameter. Defaults to the tag body (if present), or "Submit" otherwise.

Here is a submit tag example using an internationalized button label:

```
<html:submit property="btnSubmit">
  <bean:message key="label.button.submit"/>
</html:submit>
```

text

Render an HTML <input> element of type text, defaulting to the specified value or the specified property of the bean associated with the current form. This tag is valid only when nested inside an <html:form> tag body. Its attributes are listed in Table 53.

Table 53. The text tag's attributes

Attribute	Description
Common attributes	See the Common HTML Attributes and JavaScript Event Handlers.
maxlength	Maximum number of input characters to accept. Defaults to no limit.
name	The bean whose properties are consulted when rendering the current value of this input field. Defaults to the enclosing form bean if not specified.
property	Name of this input field, and the name of the corresponding bean property if value is not specified. The corresponding bean property must be of type String. (Required.)
readonly	Set to true if this input field should be read-only.
size	Approximate size (in characters) of the input box to be displayed.
value	Value to which this field should be initialized. Defaults to the value of the bean property.

The following is a typical syntax for a text tag used to build a form control for editing a bean property:

```
<html:text property="username" size="20" maxlength="20"/>
```

textarea

Render an HTML <textarea> element. This tag is valid only when nested inside an <html:form> tag body. Its attributes are listed in Table 54.

Table 54. The textarea tag's attributes

Attribute	Description
Common attributes	See the Common HTML Attributes and JavaScript Event Handlers.
cols	The number of columns to display.
name	The bean whose properties are consulted when rendering the current value of this input field. Defaults to the enclosing form bean if not specified.
property	The name of this input field, and the name of the corresponding bean property if value is not specified. The corresponding bean property must be of type String. (Required.)
readonly	Set to true if this input field should be read-only.
rows	The number of rows to display.
value	The value to which this field should be initialized. Defaults to the value of the bean property.

xhtml

Use in a page to instruct all other HTML tag library tags to render themselves as XHTML. This is useful when composing pages with JSP includes or Tiles. This tag has the same effect as using <html:html xhtml="true">. The xhtml tag has no attributes.

Logic Tags

The Struts Logic tag library contains tags (listed in Table 55) that are useful in managing conditional generation of output text, looping over object collections for repetitive generation of output text, and application flow management.

Table 55. The Logic tag library

Tag name	Description
empty	Evaluate the nested body content if the requested variable is null, an empty string, or an empty Collection or Map.
equal	Evaluate the nested body content if the requested variable is equal to a specified value.

Table 55. The Logic tag library (continued)

Tag name	Description
forward	Forward control to the page specified by an ActionForward.
greaterEqual	Evaluate the nested body content if the requested variable is greater than or equal to a specified value.
greaterThan	Evaluate the nested body content if the requested variable is greater than a specified value.
iterate	Repeat the nested body content of this tag over a specified collection.
lessEqual	Evaluate the nested body content if the requested variable is less than or equal to a specified value.
lessThan	Evaluate the nested body content if the requested variable is less than a specified value.
match	Evaluate the nested body content if a specified value is an appropriate substring of a requested variable.
messagesNotPresent	Evaluate the nested body content if a specified message is not present in the request.
messagesPresent	Evaluate the nested body content if a specified message is present in the request.
notEmpty	Evaluate the nested body content if a requested variable is neither null, an empty string, nor an empty Collection or Map.
notEqual	Evaluate the nested body content if a requested variable is not equal to a specified value.
notMatch	Evaluate the nested body content if a specified value is not an appropriate substring of a requested variable.
notPresent	Evaluate the nested body content if a specified value is not present in the request.
present	Evaluate the nested body content if a specified value is present in the request.
redirect	Render an HTTP redirect.

Because of common behavior within subsets of the Logic tags, their usage can be described using the following categories: "Value Comparison," "Empty Value Check," "Value Present Check," "Substring Matching," "Messages Check," "Application Flow Management," and "Collection Utilities."

Value Comparison

The `equal`, `notEqual`, `greaterEqual`, `greaterThan`, `lessEqual`, and `lessThan` tags render their tag body content only if a comparison you specify evaluates to true. Each of these tags supports the same set of attributes (listed in Table 56). The required `value` attribute defines one side of the comparison; you must specify exactly one of the `cookie`, `header`, `name`, or `parameter` attributes to define the other side.

You can use the `name` attribute to identify a bean that is itself the comparison variable, or use both `name` and `property` to specify a bean property.

A numeric comparison is performed if both values can be converted to a `double` or `long`; otherwise, a case-sensitive `String` comparison is performed.

The comparison returns false if a requested cookie, header, parameter, or bean property is null, but no exception is thrown. However, if both `name` and `property` are specified, an exception is thrown if the bean cannot be located.

Table 56. The value comparison tags' attributes

Attribute	Description
cookie	The case-sensitive name of a cookie to use in the comparison. Only the first value is used if multiple values exist.
header	The case-insensitive name of a header to use in the comparison. Only the first value is used if multiple values exist.
name	The name of a bean to use in the comparison. If the property attribute is also specified, the comparison is based on that bean property instead of on the bean itself.

Table 56. The value comparison tags' attributes (continued)

Attribute	Description
parameter	The case-sensitive name of a request parameter to use in the comparison. Only the first value is used if multiple values exist.
property	If name is specified, optionally specify a property of the bean to use in the comparison.
scope	The scope within which to search for the bean specified by name. If not specified, all scopes are searched.
value	The constant value to which the variable specified by the other attributes is compared. (Required.)

Here is an example of "if-else" processing using equal and notEqual with a Boolean bean property:

```
<!-- Display the "create mode" title -->
<logic:equal name="systemUserForm" property="createMode"
 value="true">
  <bean:message key="title.createSystemUser"/>
</logic:equal>

<!-- Display the "edit mode" title -->
<logic:notEqual name="systemUserForm" property="createMode"
 value="true">
  <bean:message key="title.editSystemUser"/>
</logic:notEqual>
```

The following is an example of a numeric comparison using greaterEqual:

```
<logic:greaterEqual parameter="orderTotal" value="100.00">
  <bean:message key="message.freeShipping"/>
</logic:greaterEqual>
```

Empty Value Check

The empty tag renders its nested body content only if a specified variable is null, an empty String, or an empty Collection or Map. The notEmpty tag renders its body content only if none of these conditions are true. The empty and notEmpty tags share the same attributes; they are listed in Table 57.

Table 57. The empty and notEmpty tags' attributes

Attribute	Description
name	The name of a bean to use in the comparison. If the property attribute is also specified, the comparison is based on that bean property instead of on the bean itself. (Required.)
property	Optionally specify a property of the bean identified by the name attribute to use in the comparison.
scope	The scope within which to search for the bean specified by name. If not specified, all scopes are searched.

The following example displays a title with a corresponding list of values only if the list is not empty:

```
<logic:notEmpty name="previousOrders">
  <!-- OK to display the title because at least one order
      exists -->
  <bean:message key="title.previousOrders"/>

  <ul>
    <logic:iterate id="order" name="previousOrders">
      <li><bean:write name="order"
        property="orderNumber"/></li>
    </logic:iterate>
  </ul>
<logic:notEmpty/>
```

Value Present Check

The present tag renders its nested body content only if a non-null value for a specified variable is present in the request. You must specify exactly one of the cookie, header, name, parameter, role, or user attributes to define the variable that is checked. The notPresent tag renders its content only if a non-null value for the specified variable does not exist. These tags support the same attributes, which are listed in Table 58.

You can use the name attribute to identify a bean that is itself the variable checked, or use both name and property to specify a bean property.

Table 58. The present and notPresent tags' attributes

Attribute	Description
cookie	Check for the existence of a cookie with the specified name (case-sensitive).
header	Check for the existence of an HTTP header with the specified name (case-insensitive).
name	Check for the existence of a bean with the specified name. If property is also specified, check for a non-null value for that bean property.
parameter	Check for the existence of at least one non-null value (empty string included) for the named request parameter (case-sensitive).
property	Check for the existence of a non-null property value for the bean identified by name.
role	Check whether the currently authenticated user (if any) has been associated with any of the specified security roles. Use a comma-delimited list to check several roles.
scope	The scope within which to search for the bean specified by name. If not specified, all scopes are searched.
user	Check whether the currently authenticated user principal has the specified name.

You can use the Logic present tag to guard other tags that will throw an exception if a specified variable is missing:

```
<logic:present parameter="accountNumber">
  <bean:parameter id="acctNum" name="accountNumber"/>
  <!-- Do something with the acctNum page attribute -->
</logic:present>
```

Substring Matching

The match tag renders its nested body content only if the String specified by the value attribute is a substring of the comparison variable. You must specify exactly one of the cookie, header, name, or parameter attributes to define the comparison variable. An exception is thrown if the comparison variable identified by these attributes is null. The notMatch tag renders its content only if the substring check returns false (without throwing an exception). These tags support the same attributes, which are listed in Table 59.

You can use the `name` attribute to identify a bean that is itself the comparison variable, or use both `name` and `property` to specify a bean property. A variable obtained from a bean or bean property is always converted to a `String` using `toString( )`.

Table 59. The match and notMatch tags' attributes

Attribute	Description
cookie	Compare the first (or only) value of the named cookie.
header	Compare the first (or only) value of the named header.
location	Specify `"start"` if the variable must start with the string assigned to value. Specify `"end"` to perform an endsWidth( ) comparison. If not specified, a match can occur at any position within the variable string.
name	The name of a bean to use in the comparison. If the property attribute is also specified, the comparison is based on that bean property instead of on the bean itself. (Required.)
parameter	Compare the first (or only) value of the named request parameter.
property	If name is specified, optionally specify a property of the bean to use in the comparison.
scope	The scope within which to search for the bean specified by name. If not specified, all scopes are searched.
value	The constant value that is checked for its existence as a substring of the specified variable. (Required.)

In this example, the content is rendered only if a parameter begins with a specified string:

```
<logic:matchTag parameter="action" value="update"
 location="start">
  Update in progress....
</logic:matchTag>
```

Messages Check

The messagesPresent and messagesNotPresent tags render their body content depending on the presence of general-purpose or error messages in the request. The messages are checked based on a specified or default key and can be stored using an ActionMessages object, an ActionErrors object, a String, or a String[]. These tags share the same attributes, which are listed in Table 60.

Table 60. The messagesPresent and messagesNotPresent tags' attributes

Attribute	Description
message	Set this attribute to true to check for messages in the request using Globals.MESSAGE_KEY as the key. If this attribute is true, the name attribute is ignored. Defaults to null if not specified.
name	Identify the request scope bean under which the messages have been stored. Defaults to Globals.ERROR_KEY.
property	Name of the property for which messages should be checked. If not specified, the presence of any message is checked.

The following examples show how these tags can be used to conditionally render a message list:

```
<!-- Display a formatted list of messages -->
<logic:messagesPresent message="true">
  <ul>
  <html:messages id="message" message="true"
   header="order.header"
   footer="order.footer">
    <li><bean:write name="message"/></li>
    <br>
  </html:messages>
  </ul>
</logic:messagesPresent>

<!-- No messages to display -->
<logic:messagesNotPresent message="true">
  <bean:message key="status.noNewMessages"/>
</logic:messagesNotPresent>
```

Application Flow Management

The forward and redirect tags provide control over presentation location. They are similar in function to tags found within the HTML tag library.

The forward tag performs either a forward or redirect based on the configuration of a specified global ActionForward. This tag's attribute is listed in Table 61.

Table 61. The forward tag's attribute

Attribute	Description
name	The logical name of the global ActionForward that identifies the destination and the forwarding approach. (Required.)

The redirect tag is responsible for sending a redirect to the client's browser, complete with URL-rewriting if the container supports it. Its attributes (listed in Table 62) are consistent with the link tag found in the HTML tag library. You must specify exactly one of the forward, href, or page attributes for calculation of the base URL for the redirect.

You can dynamically append parameters to the redirect URL using either one or both of the following approaches:

- Identify a bean or bean property using paramName either alone or in conjunction with paramProperty. You can optionally scope the bean name using paramScope. The value (converted to a String if necessary) is appended as a request parameter with the name given by paramId.

- Identify a bean or bean property that holds a Map of parameter names and values using name either alone or in conjunction with property. You can optionally scope the bean name using scope. Value objects other than strings and string arrays are converted using toString( ). Multiple values are passed for a parameter if a String[ ] is held in the Map.

Table 62. The redirect tag's attributes

Attribute	Description
anchor	Specify an anchor tag (without the "#") to be added to the hyperlink.
forward	Logical name of a global ActionForward that contains the content-relative URI of the destination of the redirect.
href	Absolute URL (including the protocol prefix, such as http:) to which this redirect will transfer control.
name	The name of a bean that either is a Map of query parameters itself or has a property (identified by the property attribute) that holds the desired Map.
page	The context-relative path (beginning with a "/" character) to which this redirect will transfer control.
paramId	The name of the request parameter that will be appended to the redirect URL if paramName is specified.
paramName	The name of a bean that either is a parameter value itself or has a property (identified by the paramProperty attribute) that holds the desired value.
paramProperty	Use to retrieve a parameter value from a property of the bean identified by paramName.
paramScope	The scope within which to search for the bean specified by paramName. If not specified, all scopes are searched.
property	Use to retrieve a Map of parameter values from a property of the bean identified by name.
scope	The scope within which to search for the bean specified by name. If not specified, all scopes are searched.
transaction	Set to true if you want the current transaction control token included in the generated URL.

Collection Utilities

The iterate tag executes its body content once for every element of a collection. This is particularly useful in rendering the rows of a table or sets of checkbox or radio options. Table 63 lists this tag's attribues.

You must specify either the collection or the name attribute to identify the collection to iterate. The collection attribute is for use with a runtime expression. You can use the `name` attribute to identify a bean that is itself the collection variable, or use both `name` and `property` to specify a bean property.

The collection variable you specify must be an array, a `Collection`, an `Iterator`, a `Map`, or an `Enumeration`. The `iterate` tag supports arrays of both primitives and object types.

Table 63. The iterate tag's attributes

Attribute	Description
collection	A runtime expression that evaluates to a collection.
id	The name of a page scope bean that will contain the current element of the collection on each iteration. (Required.)
indexId	The name of a page scope bean that will contain the current index of the collection on each iteration.
length	The maximum number of entries from the collection to be iterated through by the tag. You can directly specify an integer value or provide the name of an `Integer` bean (in any scope) that defines the value. Defaults to no limit.
name	The name of the bean containing the collection to be iterated (if `property` is not specified), or the bean that holds the collection as a property (if `property` is specified).
offset	The zero-relative index of the starting point within the collection for the iteration. You can directly specify an integer value or provide the name of an `Integer` bean (in any scope) that defines the value. Defaults to zero.
property	The property of the bean identified by `name` that holds the collection to be iterated.
scope	The scope within which to search for the bean specified by `name`. If not specified, all scopes are searched.
type	Fully qualified class name of the element exposed as a bean during each iteration. The elements of the collection must be assignment-compatible with this class or a `ClassCastException` will be thrown. If not specified, no type conversions are performed.

The following is an example of iterating a bean property that holds a collection:

```
<logic:iterate id="address" name="userSummary"
  property="addresses"
 type=
 "com.oreilly.struts.storefront.customer.view.AddressView">
  <tr>
    <td><bean:write name="address" property="street"/></td>
    <td><bean:write name="address" property="city"/></td>
    <td><bean:write name="address" property="state"/></td>
  </tr>
</logic:iterate>
```

In this example, the collection to be iterated is obtained by
calling the getAddresses( ) method on the userSummary bean.
During each iteration, the current AddressView object is
assigned to the address variable. Individual properties are
then retrieved from this object and displayed in a table row.

The following example uses a runtime expression to identify
a String array as the collection to iterate:

```
<% // build a test array
  String[] myCollection = {"Entry 1", "Entry 2", "Entry 3"};
%>

<table border="1">
<% String bgColor="#88EEEE"; %>

<logic:iterate id="entry" indexId="rowIndex"
 collection="<%=myCollection%>" type="java.lang.String">

  <tr bgcolor="<%=bgColor%>">
    <!-- Display the current iteration index value -->
    <td><bean:write name="rowIndex"/></td>

    <!-- Display the current element in the collection -->
    <td><bean:write name="entry"/></td>
  </tr>

  <% // use the iteration index to alternate row colors
    bgColor = (rowIndex.intValue( ) % 2 == 0) ?
      "#FFFFFF" : "#88EEEE";
  %>

</logic:iterate>
</table>
```

This example uses the `indexId` attribute to expose the current iteration index as the `rowIndex` variable. This variable is used within a tag to display its value and is also used in a scriptlet to alternate the colors of the table rows.

Nested Tags

The Struts Nested tag library allows you to use a nested object model within your pages. Most of the tags in this library are simply extensions to those found in the Bean, HTML, and Logic tag libraries. When you use a nested tag, knowledge of its enclosing parent tag allows all references to bean properties to be evaluated relative to the parent.

Even though the `form` tag is found in the HTML library, its use here provides an example of nesting:

```
<html:form action="/getUser">
  <table>
    <tr>
      <td><bean:message key="label.name"/></td>
      <td><bean:write property="userName"/></td>
    </tr>
    <tr>
      <td><bean:message key="label.city"/></td>
      <td><bean:write property="address.city"/></td>
    </tr>
    <tr>
      <td><bean:message key="label.state"/></td>
      <td><bean:write property="address.state"/></td>
    </tr>
  </table>
</html:form>
```

In this example, information is displayed about a user represented by a form bean. The table rows render their properties without having to identify the bean to which they apply. This is because the Struts framework treats the `form` tag as a parent to the tags nested within it. Any reference to a property that doesn't identify a bean is assumed to apply to the form bean. This support for nesting is limited, however.

Notice that when the address information is rendered, these references to properties deeper in the object model must repeatedly use a dot notation. The following example shows how this can be improved using nested tags:

```
<html:form action="/getUser">
  <table>
    <tr>
      <td><bean:message key="label.name"/></td>
      <td><bean:write property="userName"/></td>
    </tr>
    <nested:nest property="address">
      <tr>
        <td><bean:message key="label.city"/></td>
        <td><nested:write property="city"/></td>
      </tr>
      <tr>
        <td><bean:message key="label.state"/></td>
        <td><nested:write property="state"/></td>
      </tr>
    </nested:nest>
  </table>
</html:form>
```

In this example, the nest tag is introduced to define a nesting level for the tags it encloses. This parent tag signifies that property references made by its children will all be relative to the address property. The result is a cleaner, more object-oriented approach. Notice that the nested extension of the write tag must be used to take advantage of the nesting level. The nest tag is a child tag itself, so the address property is known to be relative to the form bean associated with the parent form tag.

If you need to access properties at a higher level in the hierarchy, a special notation based on the "/" character is supported for property names. This notation is flexible in that all that matters is the number of occurrences of the "/" character in a property name that you specify. For example, ../../address instructs the framework to move two levels up in the nesting hierarchy and access a property at that level named address. Specifying account/customer/address accomplishes the same thing in a more readable format. It is common to use either `./` or `this/` to indicate the current level. A string that starts with "/" is interpreted as starting from the root.

The nested tags can be grouped into the following categories: "Root Tags," "Nested Parent Tags," and "Child Tags."

Root Tags

The root tags (listed in Table 64) define the ultimate parent in a nested hierarchy. The bean associated with a `form` or root tag is the starting point for resolving all property references from the nested tags it encloses. You can also use `html:form` as a root. The `nested:form` tag provides the same functionality for defining a form, but its implementation is more reliable when using other nested tags.

Table 64. The root tags

Tag name	Description
form	html:form extension
root	Creates a nested hierarchy without creating a form

form

Usage of this tag is identical to `html:form`.

root

Use this tag to establish a root for a hierarchy when you don't need to create an HTML form. Its attribute is listed in Table 65.

Table 65. The root tag's attribute

Attribute	Description
name	The name of the bean from which all nested child tags will derive their bean reference.

The following example creates a hierarchy with an address bean as its root:

```
<nested:root name="address">
  <nested:write property="city"/>
</nested:root>
```

Nested Parent Tags

Nested parent tags (listed in Table 66) define another level in the hierarchy that affects the references made by the child tags they enclose. A nested parent tag cannot define the root of a hierarchy, so these tags must be used inside a form or root tag.

Table 66. The nested parent tags

Tag Name	Description
iterate	logic:iterate extension
nest	Defines a nesting level for its child tags to relate to

iterate

Iterate through a list and have all child references nest within the beans that are returned from the iteration. The attributes for this tag and their usage are identical to logic:iterate.

The following example displays a property from each element of an iteration:

```
<nested:root name="catalog">
  <!-- Iterate through the available item choices -->
  <nested:iterate id="item" property="itemChoices">

    <!-- Display a text label for this choice -->
    <nested:write property="displayLabel"/>

  </nested:iterate>
</nested:root>
```

Notice that the name property is omitted from the nested iterate tag because the nesting level defines it implicitly.

Similarly, the nested write tag does not need to reference the name exposed by the iterate tag to access a bean property.

nest

Define a new nesting level by specifying a property of the current parent. This property becomes the parent for child tags enclosed by the nest tag. Table 67 lists the attribute for this tag.

Table 67. The nest tag's attribute

Attribute	Description
property	Specify the property to which this tag and all child tags will be relative to.

The following example uses the nest tag to establish two parent levels:

```
<!-- Start with an accountView as the root -->
<nested:root name="accountView">
  <nested:write property="accountNumber"/>

  <!-- Set the account customer as the nesting level -->
  <nested:nest name="customer">
    <nested:write property="name"/>

    <!-- Set the customer address as the nesting level -->
    <nested:nest name="address">
      <nested:write property="city"/>
    </nested:nest>
  </nested:nest>
</nested:root>
```

Child Tags

The remaining nested tags (listed in Table 68) operate within the context of the current nesting level, but they are not capable of defining a new level. This is true even for tags that enclose other tags for the purpose of rendering content. For example, the select tag can be a parent to an option tag in a markup sense, but not in a nesting sense.

Most of these tags are extensions of tags in other libraries and are used in the same way as their non-nested counterparts. The only significant difference is that these nested tags can access properties of the parent tag.

Table 68. The child tags

Tag name	Description
checkbox	html:checkbox extension
define	bean:define extension
empty	logic:empty extension
equal	logic:equal extension
errors	html:errors extension
file	html:file extension
greaterEqual	logic:greaterEqual extension
greaterThan	logic:greaterThan extension
hidden	html:hidden extension
image	html:image extension
img	html:img extension
lessEqual	logic:lessEqual extension
lessThan	logic:lessThan extension
link	html:link extension
match	logic:match extension
message	bean:message extension
messages	html:messages extension
messagesNotPresent	logic:messagesNotPresent extension
messagesPresent	logic:messagesPresent extension
multibox	html:multibox extension
notEmpty	logic:notEmpty extension
notEqual	logic:notEqual extension
notMatch	logic:notMatch extension
notPresent	logic:notPresent extension

Table 68. The child tags (continued)

Tag name	Description
options	html:options extension
optionsCollection	html:optionsCollection extension
password	html:password extension
present	logic:present extension
radio	html:radio extension
select	html:select extension
size	bean:size extension
submit	html:submit extension
text	html:text extension
textarea	html:textarea extension
write	bean:write extension
writeNesting	Writes out either the current nesting level or the level defined by a property

writeNesting

Output the qualified nested name for the current nesting level or a specified level. This can be useful if you need to render a control name or JavaScript function argument that uses dot notation to fully identify the current level. Table 69 lists the writeNesting tag's attributes.

Table 69. The writeNesting tag's attributes

Attribute	Description
filter	Specify true to convert characters in the result that are sensitive in HTML. Defaults to false.
property	Specify a property reference to which the nesting level should be output. If not specified, defaults to "./" to represent the current level.

Here is an example that renders the current level:

```
<nested:nest property="createdByUser">
  <nested:nest property="firstName">
```

```
    <nested:writeNesting/>
  </nested:nest>
</nested:nest>
```

and produces the following output:

```
createdByUser.firstName
```

Tiles Tags

The Struts Tiles tag library allows you to dynamically assemble presentation pages from reusable components. This reduces the effort required to build and maintain applications in which many aspects of the presentation are common.

A tile is simply an area or region within a web page. Each tile is a JSP page that can itself be built from other tiles. The most important aspect of a tile is that it is reusable. A JSP page is typically made up of several tiles.

A *layout* is a JSP page that uses custom tags to describe the arrangement of a page. It defines what the pages of an application will look like, without specifying the content. The content is inserted into the template defined by a layout page at runtime. Layouts also are considered tiles. They can be reused by multiple JSP pages and even by multiple applications. The Tiles framework comes with several prebuilt layout tiles that you can reuse or modify as needed. The included layouts are:

Classic layout
    Renders a header, left menu, body, and footer

Columns layout
    Renders a list of tiles in multiple columns; each column renders its tiles vertically stacked

Center layout
    Renders a header, left tile, right tile, body, and footer

Menu layout
    Renders a menu with links

Tabs layout
   Renders several tiles in a tabs-like fashion

Vertical box layout
   Renders a list of tiles in a vertical column

The following JSP is an example of a custom layout tile:

```
<%@ taglib uri="/WEB-INF/struts-html.tld" prefix="html"%>
<%@ taglib uri="/WEB-INF/struts-bean.tld" prefix="bean"%>
<%@ taglib uri="/WEB-INF/tiles.tld" prefix="tiles"%>

<html:html>
 <head>
  <title><bean:message key="global.title"/></title>
  <html:base/>
 </head>
 <body topmargin="0" leftmargin="0" bgcolor="#FFFFFF">

  <!-- Header page information -->
  <tiles:insert attribute="header"/>

  <!-- Menu bar -->
  <tiles:insert attribute="menubar"/>

  <!-- Main body information -->
  <tiles:insert attribute="body-content"/>

  <!-- Copyright information -->
  <tiles:insert attribute="copyright"/>
 </body>
</html:html>
```

A layout consists of `insert` tags that determine where content is inserted at runtime. The `insert` tag performs a role similar to that of the JSP include directive. Each occurrence of this tag references a particular variable that must be supplied by the JSP using the layout. The content associated with the variable is generated and included at the location of the `insert` tag.

The following is an example of a JSP that uses the previously shown layout:

```
<%@ taglib uri="/WEB-INF/tiles.tld" prefix="tiles" %>

<tiles:insert page="/layouts/storefrontDefaultLayout.jsp"
  flush="true">
  <tiles:put name="header" value="/common/header.jsp" />
  <tiles:put name="menubar" value="/common/menubar.jsp" />
  <tiles:put name="body-content" value="/index-body.jsp" />
  <tiles:put name="copyright"
    value="/common/copyright.jsp" />
</tiles:insert>
```

The insert tag is also used in this JSP, but for a different purpose. Here the insert tag and its nested put tags are used to assign values to the variables required by the layout. The page attribute of the insert tag indicates that this JSP page is using a particular layout. The put tag is used to define the page-specific content for the template. The values of the name attribute for this tag correspond to the attributes referenced by the layout. When this JSP is executed, the page is dynamically rendered based on the layout and the attribute values.

Tiles *definitions* support another level of reuse by recognizing the fact that multiple pages in an application will likely pass the same values to a layout for certain attributes. A definition allows you to statically specify values for layout attributes that are common across pages. You can then limit the attribute values in your tiles (JSPs) to those that are actually page-specific.

Definitions can be declared in a JSP page or an XML file. The following example is a JSP definition file:

```
<%@ taglib uri="/WEB-INF/tiles.tld" prefix="tiles" %>

<tiles:definition
  id="storefront.default"
  page="/layouts/storefrontDefaultLayout.jsp"
  scope="request">
    <tiles:put name="header" value="/common/header.jsp" />
    <tiles:put name="menubar"
      value="/common/menubar.jsp" />
    <tiles:put name="copyright"
      value="/common/copyright.jsp" />
</tiles:definition>
```

This definition specifies common content for the `header`, `menubar`, and `copyright` components rendered by the layout. Individual pages that use this definition need only specify their `body-content`, as shown in the following updated JSP:

```
<%@ taglib uri="/WEB-INF/tiles.tld" prefix="tiles" %>

<%@include file="../common/storefront-defs.jsp" %>

<tiles:insert beanName="storefront.default"
 beanScope="request">
  <tiles:put name="body-content"
    value="../security/signin-body.jsp"/>
</tiles:insert>
```

You aren't limited to defining the layout attributes omitted in the definition. If you provide a value for an attribute already specified in the definition you're using, that value will override the definition.

The same definition can be defined in an XML file as:

```
<!DOCTYPE tiles-definitions PUBLIC
  "-//Apache Software Foundation//DTD Tiles Configuration//EN"
  "http://jakarta.apache.org/struts/dtds/tiles-config.dtd">
<tiles-definitions>
 <definition name="storefront.default"
   path="/layouts/storefrontDefaultLayout.jsp">
  <put name="header" value="/common/header.jsp" />
  <put name="menubar" value="/common/menubar.jsp" />
  <put name="copyright" value="/common/copyright.jsp" />
 </definition>
</tiles-definitions>
```

To use the standard definitions included in the Tiles framework, you must configure the Tiles plug-in. To add this plug-in to a Struts application, add the following element to the Struts configuration file:

```
<plug-in className="org.apache.struts.tiles.TilesPlugin" >
  <set-property property="definitions-config"
   value="/WEB-INF/tiles-defs.xml" />
  <set-property property="definitions-debug" value="2" />
  <set-property property="definitions-parser-details"
    value="2" />
```

```
    <set-property property="definitions-parser-validate"
      value="true" />
  </plug-in>
```

The property values shown here turn on configuration file validation and set the debug options to their most verbose (level 2).

Table 70 lists all of the tags in the Tiles tag library.

Table 70. The Tiles tag library

Tag name	Description
add	Add an element to an attribute value list that is being built by a putList tag.
definition	Create a definition bean.
get	Retrieve content from the request scope defined by a put tag.
getAsString	Render the value of a specified attribute to the current JspWriter.
importAttribute	Import one or all tile attributes into a specified scope.
initComponentDefinitions	Initialize tile definitions factory.
insert	Insert a tile component.
put	Put an attribute into a tile context.
putList	Declare a list that will be passed as an attribute to a tile.
useAttribute	Expose an attribute through the page context.

add

Add an element to a list being built as an attribute value. The add tag is valid only when nested inside a putList tag. You can specify the value added to the list by using the value attribute, a bean, a bean property, or the tag body.

Part of assigning an attribute value includes specifying how the value should be interpreted. An attribute value can be a literal content string, a URL that defines the content source, or a definition name. One way to specify this is by assigning one of the following values to the `type` attribute:

string
: The value is a literal content string.

page *or* template
: The value is a URL that defines the content to include.

definition
: The value is the name of a definition to use as the content source.

You can also identify the value type using the `direct` attribute. If you specify `true` for this attribute, a value type of `string` is assigned. If you specify any other non-null value for this attribute, `page` is assigned as the type. Table 71 lists the add tag's attributes.

Table 71. The add tag's attributes

Attribute	Description
beanName	The name of the bean used to retrieve the value. If beanProperty is specified, the value is retrieved from the corresponding bean property.
beanProperty	If specified, the value is retrieved from the bean property identified by beanName.
beanScope	The scope used to search for the bean identified by beanName. If not specified, all scopes are searched. (Runtime expression not allowed.)
content	This attribute is equivalent to the value attribute.
direct	An alternative to using the type attribute. Specify true to indicate that the value is literal content to be inserted directly. Specify false to indicate a reference to content to be included. Defaults to false. (Runtime expression not allowed.)
role	Specify a role name if the user must be in a specified role for the attribute value defined by this tag to be used.
type	Specify string, page, template, or definition to define the content type. (Runtime expression not allowed.)
value	Specify if not using a bean or the tag body to define the attribute value. (Runtime expression not allowed.)

See the description of the putList tag for an example that uses the add tag.

definition

The definition tag is used to create a template definition as a bean. The newly created bean is saved under the specified id in the requested scope. A definition can extend an existing definition and may overload any previously defined parameters. Table 72 lists this tag's attributes.

Table 72. The definition tag's attributes

Attribute	Description
extends	The name of a parent definition to extend.
id	The name under which the newly created definition bean will be saved. (Runtime expression not allowed.) (Required.)
page	URL of the tile/template/component to insert. Same as the template attribute.
role	The role to check before inserting this definition. If the role is not defined for the current user, the definition is not inserted. Checking is done at insertion time, not during the definition process.
scope	The variable scope in which the newly defined bean will be created. If not specified, the bean will be created in page scope. (Runtime expression not allowed.)
template	Same as the page attribute.

The following example illustrates the definition tag:

```
<tiles:definition id="storefront.default"
  page="/layouts/storefrontDefaultLayout.jsp"
    scope="request">
  <tiles:put name="header" value="/common/header.jsp" />
  <tiles:put name="menubar" value="/common/menubar.jsp" />
  <tiles:put name="copyright"
    value="/common/copyright.jsp" />
</tiles:definition>
```

get

This tag provides a subset of the functionality supported by the insert tag and is included only for compatibility with the get tag in the Struts Template tag library. It differs from insert only in that the ignore attribute defaults to true for this tag.

getAsString

Retrieve the String value of the specified tile attribute and render it to the current JspWriter. The usual toString( ) conversion is applied to the value. Table 73 lists this tag's attributes.

Table 73. The getAsString tag's attributes

Attribute	Description
ignore	Set to true to return without error if the named attribute does not exist. Otherwise, a runtime exception is thrown in this case. Defaults to false.
name	The attribute name. (Required.)
role	Specify a role name if the user must be in a specified role for this tag to execute.

In the following example, getAsString is used to directly insert the page title into a layout tile:

```
<html>
  <head>
    <title><tiles:getAsString name="pageTitle"/></title>
  </head>
</html>
```

importAttribute

Import a named attribute (or all attributes) from the current tile context into a specified scope. The name and scope attributes are optional. If not specified, all tile attributes are imported into page scope. Once imported, you can access a tile attribute as a bean using non-tiles tags. This tag is similar to useAttribute, but it does not create scripting variables and does not allow you to specify a new name for an attribute. The importAttribute tag's attributes are listed in Table 74.

Table 74. The importAttribute tag's attributes

Attribute	Description
ignore	Set to true to return without error if the named attribute does not exist. Otherwise, a runtime exception is thrown in this case. Defaults to false.
name	The name of the tile attribute to import. If not specified, all attributes within the current context are imported.
scope	Scope of the imported attribute(s). Defaults to "page". (Runtime expression not allowed.)

Here is an example of importing all attributes into the page context and checking for a particular one:

```
<tiles:importAttribute/>
<logic:present name="menubar">
  Menubar content was imported!
</logic:present>
```

initComponentDefinitions

Initialize the definitions factory. This is typically done in an initialization servlet, but can also be done using this tag. Its attributes are listed in Table 75.

Table 75. The initComponentDefinitions tag's attributes

Attribute	Description
classname	Fully qualified class name of the factory to create and initialize. (Runtime expression not allowed.)
file	The definition configuration file name. (Runtime expression not allowed.) (Required.)

insert

Insert content into a page. In a layout tile, the insert tag uses attribute values to prescribe where the content will go. In a regular, nonlayout tile, the `insert` tag is used to retrieve a layout and allow content to be passed to the layout using put tags. Table 76 lists the `insert` tag's attributes.

Table 76. The insert tag's attributes

Attribute	Description
attribute	The name of an attribute in the current tile context to insert. (Runtime expression not allowed.)
beanName	The name of a bean to be used in retrieving the content.
beanProperty	If specified, the name of the property to retrieve from the bean identified by beanName.
beanScope	The scope used to search for the bean identified by beanName. If not specified, all scopes are searched. (Runtime expression not allowed.)
component	A string representing the URI of a tile or template. The component, page, and template attributes have exactly the same behavior.
controllerClass	The class type of a controller called immediately before the page is inserted. The controller is used to prepare data to be rendered by the inserted tile. Only one of controllerUrl or controllerClass should be used.
controllerUrl	The URL of a controller called immediately before the page is inserted. The URL usually denotes a Struts action.
definition	The name of the definition to insert. Currently, only definitions from a factory can be inserted with this attribute. Use the beanName attribute to insert a definition created using the definition tag.
flush	Set to true to flush the current page output stream before tile insertion. (Runtime expression not allowed.)
ignore	Set to true to return without error if the named attribute does not exist. Otherwise, a runtime exception is thrown in this case. Defaults to false.
name	The name of an entity to insert. The search is done in this order: definition, attribute, and then page.

Table 76. The insert tag's attributes (continued)

Attribute	Description
page	A string representing the URI of a tile or template. The component, page, and template attributes have exactly the same behavior.
role	Specify a role name if the user must be in a specified role for this tag to execute.
template	A string representing the URI of a tile or template. The component, page, and template attributes have exactly the same behavior.

The following example illustrates a typical use of insert to define content passed to a layout tile:

```
<tiles:insert page="/layouts/storefrontDefaultLayout.jsp">
  <tiles:put name="header" value="/common/header.jsp"
    type="page"/>
  <tiles:put name="body-content" value="/index-body.jsp" />
</tiles:insert>
```

The following is an example of inserting content using a definition created with the definition tag:

```
<tiles:insert beanName="storefront.default"
  beanScope="request">
  <tiles:put name="body-content"
    value="../security/signin-body.jsp"/>
</tiles:insert>
```

This example specifies an attribute to retrieve and render content in a layout tile:

```
<tiles:insert attribute="body-content"/>
```

put

Assign an attribute value to be passed to a tile component. The put tag is valid only when nested inside an insert or definition tag. You can specify the value using the value attribute, a bean, a bean property, or the tag body.

Part of assigning an attribute value includes specifying how the value should be interpreted. An attribute value can be a literal content string, a URL that defines the content source, or a definition name. One way to specify this is by assigning one of the following values to the type attribute:

string
   The value is a literal content string.

page *or* template
   The value is a URL that defines the content to include.

definition
   The value is the name of a definition to use as the content source.

You can also identify the value type using the direct attribute. If you specify true for this attribute, a value type of string is assigned. If you specify any other non-null value for this attribute, page is assigned as the type. Table 77 lists the put tag's attributes.

Table 77. The put tag's attributes

Attribute	Description
beanName	The name of the bean used to retrieve the value.
beanProperty	If specified, the value is retrieved from the bean property identified by beanName.
beanScope	The scope used to search for the bean identified by beanName. If not specified, all scopes are searched. (Runtime expression not allowed.)
content	This attribute is equivalent to the value attribute.
direct	An alternative to using the type attribute. Specify true to indicate that the value is literal content to be inserted directly. Specify false to indicate a reference to content to be included. Defaults to false. (Runtime expression not allowed.)
name	The name of the attribute. (Runtime expression not allowed.) (Required.)
role	Specify a role name if the user must be in a specified role for the attribute value defined by this tag to be used.

Table 77. The put tag's attributes (continued)

Attribute	Description
type	Specify string, page, template, or definition to define the content type. (Runtime expression not allowed.)
value	Specify if not using a bean or the tag body to define the attribute value.

Here is an example of assigning a page URL:

```
<tiles:insert page="/layouts/storefrontDefaultLayout.jsp">
  <tiles:put name="header" value="/common/header.jsp"
    type="page"/>
</tiles:insert>
```

putList

Create a list to pass as an attribute value to a tile. This tag supports attributes that accept values of type java.util.List. Rather than directly supporting insert tags in another tile, list values may instead be intended for attributes imported into a page and accessed using other tags. For example, you might want to include a logic:iterate tag in a layout that defines how the rows of a table should be rendered.

The list elements are added using the add tag. The putList tag can be used only inside an insert or definition tag. Its attribute is listed in Table 78.

Table 78. The putList tag's attribute

Attribute	Description
name	Name of the list. (Runtime expression not allowed.) (Required.)

Here is an example of putList and its nested add tags:

```
<tiles:insert page="/layouts/headlinesLayout.jsp">
  <tiles:putList name="categories">
    <tiles:add direct="true">
      <bean:message key="title.financial"/>
    </tiles:add>
```

```
    <tiles:add direct="true">
      <bean:message key="title.sports"/>
    </tiles:add>
  </tiles:putList>
</tiles:insert>
```

useAttribute

Expose a scripting variable and an attribute in a specified scope based on the value of a tile attribute. The variable and attribute will have the name specified by id, or by the tile attribute name if not specified. This tag allows you to reference an attribute associated with a tile from other non-tiles tags. Table 79 lists the useAttribute tag's attributes.

Table 79. The useAttribute tag's attributes

Attribute	Description
classname	The fully qualified class name of the declared scripting variable. If not specified, the variable is treated as an Object. (Runtime expression not allowed.)
id	Declared attribute and variable name. Defaults to the tile attribute name. (Runtime expression not allowed.)
ignore	Set to true to return without error if the named attribute does not exist. Otherwise, a runtime exception is thrown in this case. Defaults to false.
name	The tile attribute name. (Required.)
scope	Scope of the created attribute. Defaults to "page". (Runtime expression not allowed.)

The following is an example of accessing a tile attribute from a Bean tag:

```
<!-- Expose a tile attribute and display its value -->
<tiles:useAttribute name="title"/>
<bean:write name="title"/
```

PART V

Resources

This part provides a list of resources that you can use to quickly look up further information on Struts and its supporting technologies.

The Struts Mailing Lists

The best places to learn and ask questions about the Struts framework are the two Struts mailing lists: *STRUTS-USER* and *STRUTS-DEV*. The user list currently has around 1,750 subscribers and has been growing at a rate of 50 to 100 new users each month for the past year or so.

To subscribe to these lists, visit *http://jakarta.apache.org/ struts/learning.html*.

There are also several ways to search these mailing lists. The Mail Archive is a good place to search through many Jakarta mailing lists, not just those dedicated to Struts. Use the URL *http://www.mail-archive.com/index.php?hunt=struts* and select either the development list or the user list. You can also use the *eyebrowse* feature from the Apache Software Foundation to search these lists. You can use *eyebrowse* online at *http:// nagoya.apache.org/eyebrowse*.

Another site that allows you to search the Struts DEV and USER lists can be found at *http://marc.theaimsgroup.com*.

The Struts Resource Web Page

There are several interesting and informative links on the Struts web site. The Struts Resource Page (*http://jakarta.apache.org/ struts/resources/index.html*) is a good starting place. This list is divided by category, and you can easily spend a solid month following all of these links.

Struts Tools

Several Struts GUI tools are available, with more being created every day. Some have no financial cost associated with them, whereas others can be cost prohibitive. The following table lists several tools that you can evaluate.

Name	URL
Adalon	*http://www.synthis.com*
Easy Struts	*http://easystruts.sourceforge.net*
MDE for Struts	*http://www.metanology.com*
Struts Console	*http://www.jamesholmes.com*

You can find a more complete (and always current) list on the Struts tools page at *http://jakarta.apache.org/struts/ resources/tools.html*.

Index

We'd like to hear your suggestions for improving our indexes. Send email to
index@oreilly.com.

Learn from experts.
Find the answers you need.

Sign up for a **10-day free trial** to get **unlimited access** to all of the
content on Safari, including Learning Paths, interactive tutorials,
and curated playlists that draw from thousands of ebooks and
training videos on a wide range of topics, including data, design,
DevOps, management, business—and much more.

Start your free trial at:
oreilly.com/safari

(No credit card required.)

Lightning Source UK Ltd.
Milton Keynes UK
UKHW02f0625090318
319123UK00006B/336/P